JOHN GUNN

TALES
FROM THE
TOUCHLINE

Football Memories from
a Referee and Fan

First published by Pitch Publishing, 2021

Pitch Publishing
A2 Yeoman Gate
Yeoman Way
Worthing
Sussex
BN13 3QZ
www.pitchpublishing.co.uk
info@pitchpublishing.co.uk

A CIP catalogue record is available for this book
from the British Library.

ISBN 978-1 78531 818 4

Typesetting and origination by Pitch Publishing
Printed and bound in India by Replika Press Pvt. Ltd.

Contents

To Mike
Best Wishes

John Aum (signature)

TALES
FROM THE
TOUCHLINE

ACKNOWLEDGEMENTS

THERE ARE quite a few people I would like to thank for the help they have given me to complete this publication.

Mr Reid, my English teacher at school many years ago, whose guidance and confidence in my ability stays with me to this day.

Big Yorkshire pal and staunch Leeds United fan Stevie Sharp, for giving me the idea and inspiration to eventually get round to writing the book.

The delightful Laura Coventry, friend and journalist colleague, for doing all the proofreading and giving me the benefit of her editorial experience.

My guide and refereeing mentor, Sandy Roy, for looking over the accuracy of the refereeing element of the tales.

Mike Watson, friend and fellow Dundee United fan, for his help with information on United for Change events.

Last, but not least, my lovely wife Sheila, for driving me on to achieve a lifelong ambition. Without her encouragement and patience this book would not have been possible.

INTRODUCTION

I WAS born in the Fair City of Perth on 23 April 1956, the eldest son to my parents, John and Margaret, two of the nicest and hardest-working people to have graced this earth. My brother Neil is 20 months my junior. Although starting my life just outside Crieff in rural Perthshire before moving to Dundee, I regard myself very much as a Dundonian, if not by birth then by adoption.

Educated to 'O' Grade standard, I was far more interested in football to be bothered with studying for exams, although I did gain As in English and Arithmetic and Cs in French and History. What could I have achieved if I had tried a little harder?

The one subject which came naturally to me was English. I won prizes for composition on a regular basis and when I decided to leave school at 16, my teacher Mr Reid urged me to stay on and take my

Higher English with a view to carving out a career in journalism. All I wanted to do, however, was get out to work and earn some money.

Throughout my time at school I played as much football as I could, competing at primary, under-13, under-16 and boys' club level on either a Saturday or Sunday, or often both. I was a decent full-back, although nothing special, and did captain my under-16 team and played against guys who went on to make excellent careers in the game, such as future Scotland internationals Paul Sturrock (Dundee United) and Jim Blyth (Coventry City).

On leaving school I embarked on a career with publisher DC Thomson as an apprentice compositor, working on the *Dundee Evening Telegraph* (the next best thing to becoming a journalist). I have been in and out of the newspaper industry all of my working life, moving briefly to Elgin and then to Aberdeen where I lived for 32 years.

In 2017 I relocated to Glasgow where I have now gone full circle, returning to DC Thomson, now known as DCT Media, as an advertising sales consultant with *The Sunday Post*.

My obsession with Dundee United Football Club continued to grow, taking in the Scandinavian era in the mid-1960s to the glory days of winning the league and European ties in the 1980s and up to the present day. I have been a season ticket holder at Tannadice since retiring from the SFA Senior List of Referees in the 1990s.

When I was living in Elgin in the late 1970s there was no Saturday amateur football to play, I didn't fancy playing in the local Sunday league, and was certainly not good enough to play at Junior or Highland League level, so when I saw an article in the local paper looking for new referees to start a course in a few weeks, I jumped at the chance and never looked back.

Starting off at schools and boys' club level, progressing to become a Highland League linesman, I was then fast-tracked to become a referee in the North Region Junior League in a short space of time. After spending three-and-a-half seasons at that level I was then promoted to the SFA Senior List in June 1984 where I served for ten seasons as a Highland League referee and an SFL and SPL linesman.

After retirement from the Senior List I continued to referee in the Aberdeen Sunday Welfare League for a couple of years, while watching my beloved Dundee United on a Saturday, until I retired completely to help form and run a Sunday Welfare team in my home town of Portlethen, on the outskirts of the Granite City. I also served on the executive committee of the Welfare League, eventually becoming chairman for three years.

My stories to tell are controversial, factual, and, I hope, delivered with a great deal of humour. I hope you enjoy reading this book as much as I have enjoyed writing it.

1

FROM PLAYING
TO REFEREEING

MY FOOTBALL playing career was somewhat non-existent, but I do have a couple of memories from my school days where I ended up captaining my team at under-16 level.

As already mentioned, I was a decent full-back and having a bit of pace tried to get forward as much as I could, as overlapping full-backs were the fashion of that period in the early 1970s. But during one match against Stanley Secondary School my gym teacher Dougie McRae decided to play me on the wing because of my speed. That day I scored the only hat-trick I ever achieved, whether it be in a competitive match or a kick-about with my mates in the playground.

Also, it was the perfect threesome would you believe – right foot, left foot and a header. I remember it as if it were yesterday! My partner up front was my best mate Andy Smith, who was not as fast as me and a good bit shorter, but a damn good player. We played really well together, me assisting in his two goals and Andy laying on the passes for the two of mine with my feet. However, it was my header which had an air of comedy about it.

Our goalkeeper Norrie McLellan punted a long ball upfield with Andy on the chase and me alongside him. The wee man managed to get the ball under control as their goalkeeper had come out to narrow the angle and I was totally unmarked, screaming for a pass inside. Andy, also looking for his hat-trick, had other ideas. He continued bearing down on goal but only succeeded in colliding with the keeper. With the ball spinning up in the air towards me, I had the simplest of tasks to nod it between the unguarded posts (no nets in these days!). One happy Gunner and one sheepish-looking Smithy.

The other incident I recall was totally bizarre. We were playing a cup semi-final against St Columba's High School from Perth when Norrie McLellan inexplicably did not turn up. As the final was due to be played at Muirton Park, Perth, the then home of St Johnstone FC who played in the top division in Scotland, this was a very big game for all the lads and Norrie not turning up was unforgivable.

I was selected to play in goal by Dougie McRae. I had, on occasion, played there before so I was not particularly fazed about doing so again in such an important game.

St Columba's were a very good side, marshalled by an excellent captain in Drew Melley, and they raced into an early three-goal lead. We fought back to go in at the interval 3-2 down. The second half was an end-to-end affair and, with a couple of minutes to go, the score was tied at 6-6 when St Columba's were awarded a penalty.

This was a very nerve-wracking moment for me as the guy taking the penalty was their tricky left-winger named Nicky Mulligan, who only had one arm. Despite his disability the lad had tremendous balance and a deadly left foot. The referee blew his whistle and up Mulligan stepped to side-foot the ball well to my right-hand side. I went down on one knee as a token gesture as I was never going to reach it, but the ball hit the inside of the post, spun across goal, skimmed my head on the way past, hit the inside of the other post, came back across, hit my left leg and trickled over the line. That was the final goal in the game and the chance to play at Muirton Park was gone. Absolutely gutted!

When I started out with the *Dundee Evening Telegraph* I was required to work on Saturdays, so that put paid to any designs I may have had about playing at any decent level, although I did play a few games in a Sunday juvenile league.

One game stands out in particular as I was getting an absolute roasting from a left-winger called Jimmy Robertson, who played for Newburgh Juveniles. The referee that day was a great guy called Willie Doig, who had the knack of talking to the players and getting the best out of them. Jimmy was far too quick and skilful for me and I took him down a few times before being called over by Willie, who said, 'Aye laddie, enjoying your game today?' I replied, 'No I bloody well wasn't,' due to wee Jimmy turning me inside out. 'Well, just a wee word of warning, any more fouls and you will find your name going into my book.' Fair enough, I thought.

In the second half and, after another couple of fouls, Willie, quite rightly, shouted me across to give me a caution. 'Right, laddie,' he said, 'you really are going to have to watch yourself now. Maybe you should have a word with your bench to see if it is worth your while continuing.' One foul on Jimmy later and I was quickly substituted for my own good.

I glanced across to Willie, who was smiling and winked at me with a thumbs-up sign as he trotted back up the field. The lesson I took from that game was that Willie Doig knew Jimmy Robertson had me on toast that day, but he also knew that I wasn't a dirty player, just not good enough to stop him by fair means on the day. He didn't want to send me off and was quite happy to see me substituted before he really had to dismiss me.

By this time, I realised that perhaps my playing days should come to an end fairly quickly.

* * *

I moved to Elgin from Dundee in 1979 and, as it was a local weekly newspaper group I was employed by, I did not work on Saturdays. This was a bit of a culture shock to me as I was now able to go and watch football again. If Elgin City, the local Highland League team at that time, were at home I would invariably go to watch them as they had quite a good side. If they were away I would go and have a look at one of the three local junior sides – Bishopmill United, New Elgin or Caberfeidh, who played on the pitch next to my house.

One July day that year I happened to pick up a bit of copy for the newspaper I worked with, *The Northern Scot*, which needed to be typeset, now my occupation. It was a piece from the local SFA Referees' Association looking for new recruits to come on a 13-week course with a view to becoming a qualified referee at the end of it.

As it happened my uncle, Ali Gunn, had been a referee in the Tayside Amateur FA for many years and I also knew Grade 1 official Bob Valentine very well, having worked alongside him in Dundee. I thought to myself, 'I would love to have a crack at this. There is nowhere for you to play up here and you're not very good anyway!' So, I applied for a place on the course with the then secretary, David Simpson, and the rest, as they say, is history.

I was invited by David to attend training sessions in August before the course started in September and was introduced to my new colleagues including Sandy Roy, Robbie Harrold, George Newlands, Bob Stuart, Gordon Logan, Robbie Russell, Ali MacDonald, Sandy Smith, Robbie Ness and Stuart Logan among quite a few others. The group at that time was the SFA

North of Scotland Referees' Association which covered an area from Wick in the north, Fort William in the west to Banff in the east. Far too big a geographical area to function properly, I thought, and this was to change within the next couple of years.

The course was run by Robbie Harrold and I found it very interesting indeed as there were quite a few little technical points within the 17 Laws of the Game which I thought I knew all about but quite obviously did not. The two-hour exam, which required an 80 per cent pass mark, took place a couple of weeks before Christmas and I found out in January that I had passed with flying colours.

I continued to referee schools' football, which I had started doing the previous September, and officiated as a linesman at various youth levels in cup semi-finals and finals. In early March I was informed that I would be getting a few games as a linesman at some end of the season Highland League fixtures. My first match was Nairn County versus Forres Mechanics where the home side ran out 2-1 winners. This was the beginning of a nice wee journey.

During that summer I was cutting my teeth in the local amateur and welfare leagues – Elgin & District, Buckie & District and Speyside – and in August at the beginning of the 1980/81 Highland League season I was to become a regular linesman at its matches.

One highlight from the Elgin & District Amateur League involved making a decision which would have been frowned upon by any referee supervisor had they been present. There were two pitches used by the league in Elgin, lying between the housing estates of Bishopmill and South Lesmurdie, which were situated in a very large area of grassland. There was a little guy who played for Elgin Cosmos whose first name I can only remember as being 'Alfie'. He was a cocky little character and not too bad a player. I had previously given him a yellow card in a game where he was about to take the kick-off after the half-time break while smoking the last draw of his cigarette!

On this occasion I had awarded a free kick against him for tripping an opponent, then he deliberately booted the ball as far as he could away from the pitch. Normally I would have cautioned him immediately, but I had another form of punishment to administer. I called him over and let him have a look at the yellow card in my hand and said, 'Take your pick son, either you go and get the ball or I give you a card.' Alfie immediately retorted, 'You wouldn't dare!' as he looked across to his manager, who was having a good laugh about the situation on the touchline, for some sort of guidance. Our eyes then met again and as I stared him out, very slowly lifting my card to mete out his 'proper' punishment, he started to sprint to retrieve the ball. Card back in pocket, job done and no more bother from Alfie that Sunday afternoon!

I had been informed by some of my more experienced colleagues that I had been progressing quite well as a referee and that if I continued to improve then I could go far in the game. I hadn't really thought about promotion through the ranks as I had only taken up refereeing to be involved in football on a regular basis. But then I started to listen more intently to the conversations at training among the guys on the SFA Senior List and heard their tales of trips to Pittodrie, Tannadice, East End Park, Tynecastle and the like and decided that I would like a piece of that action as well.

I was thoroughly enjoying the start to my refereeing career and in the main was quite pleased with the majority of my performances when one Tuesday night around October time I was approached after training by Robbie Harrold and Sandy Roy. My immediate thought was, 'What have I done?' but big Sandy soon put my mind at rest. He informed me that there was a shortage of referees at junior level and it was thought by Robbie and himself, among others, that I was good enough to take that step up, but they wanted to know how I felt about it. Under normal circumstances I would not even have been considered for promotion until the start of the next season at the very earliest but, as these two experienced campaigners had faith in my ability and I now had the burning desire to move up through the ranks, I decided to give it a go. It was a decision I never regretted.

2

JUNIOR FOOTBALL

I SPENT three and a half fantastic years refereeing in the North Region (North Section) League and have some great memories from those days.

As I had been quite highly regarded by some of the top brass in north junior football, I was given quite a few tasty Scottish Junior Cup ties to referee throughout my time as well. Jim Grant, who was chairman of Burghead Thistle and the local Junior Association, later to become president of the Scottish Junior FA, was my main ally along with Sandy Logie from Forres Thistle, Bill Cruickshank from Islavale, the local association secretary Ben Strachan and the doyen of them all – league treasurer and north football legend William 'Wick' Allan, who also became a big influence on my career.

I recall one game between Burghead and Forres at Forest Park where the home side had two cousins playing for them but they actually looked like identical twins. There was a serious incident involving one of them, a bit of a scuffle took place after it and I called one of the cousins over to dish out a red card for his part.

After the game I was in my dressing room when there was a knock at the door. Jim and Sandy were standing there and asked if they could come in. 'Absolutely no problem, how can I help?' I replied. Jim then said, 'I am afraid you sent off the wrong laddie, it was his cousin who kicked the Forres player.' I immediately glanced at Sandy, who concurred with Jim's statement.

Now, these gentlemen were two of the most honest and upstanding guys I had ever met in the game and it became pretty obvious to me that I had made a genuine mistake. After pausing for a few moments I took my notebook out of my pocket, crossed off the player's name, number and time of the incident, thanked Jim and Sandy for their time and as I opened the door to let them out Jim turned and said softly, 'Of course, John, this conversation never took place.' Enough said. The main thing that bothered me about the whole episode was the fact that the real culprit got away with his misdemeanour as I could not retrospectively send him off.

Around about this time it was decided that referees based in the counties of Moray and Banff would break away from the SFA North of Scotland Referees' Association to form their own group. This was ratified by the SFA in 1981 as the previous area was too large to handle for one group. I am proud to say I am a founder member of the SFA Moray and Banff Referees' Association where I spent four years before my move to Aberdeen. I occupied a number of committee positions including match secretary and vice-president to Sandy Roy. We were the smallest association in the country as far as personnel was concerned but we were quite a tight-knit group and I have great memories of my time there and made some good friends.

There were a few characters I came across in junior football who would either brighten my day or totally spoil it. One such individual who loved to perform the latter was Graham Tatters, an RAF serviceman at Kinloss who played for the base team in the North Section Junior League. Tatters was one of the biggest and loudest moaners of his generation. He was quite an intelligent guy who would try to baffle you with his words of wisdom, thinking he could talk his way out of trouble. Never once did it work.

He was a decent whole-hearted player, without being brilliant, who later moved on to play for Elgin side Bishopmill United and continued to give officials GBH of the earhole on a weekly basis. I remember one local derby against New Elgin where their tricky winger Mark George was giving Graham a bit of a hard time. After one foul too many I called him across to administer a yellow card. Before I could do so he, as usual, tried to sweet talk his way out of it. I told him to shut up but he continued to argue his case. It was then I decided to give him a choice. I took my yellow and red cards from my pocket and said, 'Mr Tatters, you have a decision to make: you can cease arguing now and I will only show you my yellow card or you can continue with your dissent and I will show you my red card.' Being the arrogant sod he was, he continued, probably thinking I would not have the balls to carry out my threat. I issued a yellow card for the foul, a red for the dissent and sent him from the field of play where he continued to mutter his discontent at my decision.

As a player he never changed and every referee had problems with him, but he was an intelligent person and later went on to take up the position of team manager with Lossiemouth, eventually ending up as chairman of Elgin City after they gained Scottish League status. His heart was always in the right place, he just couldn't keep his mouth shut.

Wick Allan was in his 80s when I started in the junior leagues, an ex-Highland League goalkeeper who, after his playing career, became a very good referee. Despite his age Wick was as sharp as a tack and his eyesight was impeccable. He made it his mission to advise and encourage up-and-coming referees in the junior ranks to further their careers. Every Thursday or Friday evening Wick would telephone one of the junior officials to ask if he could accompany them to their game on the Saturday.

I know for a fact that this made some of my colleagues feel uncomfortable as he was renowned for his direct approach and did not mince his words when it came to critical comments about performances. I was the opposite. Being of the same nature as Wick, I welcomed any constructive criticism which would help me further my career. Despite his forthright manner in assessing referees' performances, Wick was a lovely man, mild-mannered with a dry sense of humour, and he loved a 'wee dram'.

As I had ambition and a willingness to learn and improve, Wick took a shine to me and we became good friends. He could see the potential in me and really wanted me to succeed. My colleagues who did not listen to his advice would not get the same attention and, for that reason, their careers would go no further. One of them, Ian McHattie, was criticising Wick after training one Tuesday night about his comments following his game on the previous Saturday. He was giving the impression that he knew better than Wick and dismissed his comments out of hand. I advised McHattie that he was making a big mistake if he did not listen to a man who had a lifetime's experience in the game compared to his own short, so far uneventful, career.

I came across quite a few referees over the years who thought they were a lot better than most of their colleagues and deserved to get promoted through the ranks when, in fact, they were not that good at all. McHattie fell into that category and I think he gave up refereeing quite early as it was obvious he wasn't going to progress, no doubt blaming every man and his granny apart from himself for his demise. Lesson – always listen to the voice of experience.

Wick continued to help me as I gained more and more games under my belt and became able to handle certain situations in a different way down to his words of wisdom. I was beginning to earn a reputation with the teams that, although approachable and having a common-sense attitude, I would not stand for any nonsense and would deliver appropriate punishment when necessary.

I was also getting appointed to quite a few of the top league and cup games in the North Section and officiated at some tasty Scottish Junior Cup ties involving well-known teams from the South of Scotland such as Pollok, Shettleston, Irvine Meadow, Lesmahagow and Benburb.

One October Saturday in 1983 was very special for me when I was appointed to referee a tie in Elgin between Bishopmill United and Coltness United from Lanarkshire. On the same day New Elgin were at home to Balbeggie Juniors from my homeland Tayside League. The away side's chairman was my uncle, Ali, who had long since hung up his whistle and gone into administrative roles within the game.

Northern clubs are well known for their hospitality and would always invite their opponents back to a local social club or pub for a bite to eat and a few refreshments. I asked Robbie Nicol, manager of New Elgin, if it would be okay to come up to their establishment, The Golden Pheasant, after I completed my duties at Borough Briggs, so that I could have a beer with my uncle. That was never going to be a problem and I saw Uncle Ali for the last time. He hadn't been keeping too well and had recently been through major surgery, but he was delighted to see me and I got the impression he was quite proud that I was progressing through the refereeing ranks. I thoroughly enjoyed spending a bit of time with him regaling tales of my experiences so far. Sadly, he passed away a few months later.

Coming towards the end of the 1982/83 season I had been doing very well and was being touted for promotion to the SFA Senior List along with a Moray and Banff colleague of mine, Gordon Hines, who had one year's more experience than me in the junior ranks. Being based in Elgin, referees who were looking to step up a grade quite often had to officiate at matches outside of their own area.

One Tuesday evening Gordon and I were both appointed to referee matches in Aberdeen. He was to do East End v Parkvale and I had Sunnybank v Mugiemoss, both in the North Region (East Section) Division One. Now, at that time, the Aberdeen & District Referees' Association only had one supervisor,

Bert Sturgeon, so how both of us were going to be covered seemed very unlikely unless someone was to come up from Dundee.

As it turned out Sturgeon went to have a look at Gordon and my game was not covered. I was very disappointed as the match I refereed was very important to the eventual destination of the league title. As Mugiemoss needed to win and Sunnybank only required a draw it had all the ingredients for a tough encounter. It did, indeed, turn out that way and after a pulsating end-to-end contest Sunnybank emerged 3-2 winners. I felt I had a good game and was told so by the losing manager, Tommy Cummings, who later went on to take care of Cove Rangers in the Highland League and was also a very successful Aberdeen businessman. I shared a few beers with Tommy over the years after my move to Aberdeen.

Gordon picked me up in his car and on the way home we both discussed our games. He thought he had done okay but nothing spectacular, but as he was quite a quiet, introverted character I took it with a pinch of salt. He was a good referee and nice guy, after all, and was genuinely disappointed for me when I informed him there wasn't a supervisor at my game. He then questioned why we had both been sent through to the Granite City when our own supervisor, by this time Robbie Harrold, must have known that only one of us was going to be assessed. My view at the time was that, as Gordon had more experience than me, it was him that was being pushed and I was sent through just for the experience. I didn't really complain as it was a good test and it would be extremely unlikely that two junior referees from the smallest association in the country would be promoted at the same time.

A week later I informed the association I was taking a week's holiday with my family at my parents' home on Tayside. When Harrold got to hear of this, he said he would get me a game in the Tayside Junior League and would make sure a supervisor covered it. The fixture I was given to referee was Kirrie Thistle v Lochee United on 14 May (what a day that was going to turn out to be!), so I gave the Tayside secretary my mum and dad's phone number in case anything went wrong.

Maybe I was wrong, maybe there still was a chance of getting promotion after all. I was really looking forward to the game, despite the fact there was another very important fixture taking place at Dens Park on the same afternoon between Dundee and local rivals United on the last day of the Scottish Premier League season. If United won they would be league champions and I was going to miss it, or so I thought.

On the morning of the match I was only focussed on what lay ahead of me later in the day when, suddenly, the phone rang. My dad answered, then passed it to me, saying, 'It's for you.' It was the secretary of the Tayside Juniors who was calling to inform me that because of heavy rainfall over the last few days my game at Kirriemuir was postponed as the pitch was waterlogged. There were quite a few other junior games called off that day for the same reason.

The first thing I had to do was telephone Harrold to let him know about the situation. He was not best pleased as he had organised for a supervisor to be present at my game. I could hardly be held responsible for the weather, could I?

It was now sinking in that my chances of promotion were now pretty slim as there were very few games left in the season. As it turned out Gordon Hines moved up a grade and I would have to wait another year. Despite being a little bit disappointed I realised that another year refereeing junior football would stand me in good stead.

But never mind all that, was the Dundee derby going ahead? Although the pitch was very heavy it was *y*able and as the match was not all ticket I

y to Thomsons Bar to meet my pals before

to Dens.

The ground was jam-packed that day. I stood in what was known as the T.C. Keay End for what seemed an eternity. United were attacking that goal in the first half and raced to a 2-0 lead before there were 15 minutes on the clock. Ralph Milne, with a delightful chip over the Dundee keeper, and Eamonn Bannon, with a follow-up shot from his saved penalty, were the scorers. Ian Ferguson scored for Dundee before half-time.

The second half was the longest I ever endured as a fan. There was a large clock behind me and I think I cricked my neck by turning round to have a look every two minutes and willing it to move quicker.

The fixture finished 2-1 and United were champions for the first time in their history, an absolutely fantastic achievement for a club of its size. It was party time!

The 1983/84 season was a bit of a blur for me as I seemed to be doing two games just about every week. The experience I gained helped me enormously in my quest to gain promotion at the end of that campaign. I officiated at quite a few cup finals and had the honour of travelling through to Aberdeen for a representative match between a North Junior Select and a Tayside Junior Select, and I was a linesman at a North Junior Select against Scotland Juniors fixture.

I was fairly confident that, based on my overall performances and the good reports I had received from supervisors, I would get promotion to the SFA Senior List.

One of the highlights of the refereeing calendar was the annual conference held at the University of St Andrews every June. It was more of a social gathering than anything else but that was when the SFA Referee Supervisors' Committee made their decisions on promotions and demotions for the next season. I had been tipped off that I had been promoted and it made for a great weekend.

The conference weekends were a fantastic experience. We had the opportunity to meet many of the top officials from throughout the country, informally discussing all topics refereeing or anything else football-related, accompanied by a considerable amount of alcoholic refreshments, of course. In those days I was slim and fit and had a reputation for downing several pints of lager with it having little or no effect on my personality. For that reason, I was christened 'Hollow Legs' by some of my colleagues.

We used to frequent several establishments in the university town, but my favourite watering hole was The Jigger, which was on the edge of the famous home of golf, The Old Course. Some serious drinking took place in there and it was where I met a freelance journalist from Dundee called Dick Donnelly.

Dick was a former professional goalkeeper who had played for East Fife many years previously, and I just loved being in his company as he had an endless amount of stories to tell. The more whisky you supplied him with the more you got out of him. A brilliant character.

Over the years the annual conferences' heavy social side was frowned upon by the powers that be and it became more of a coaching weekend, although that did not deter the guys who liked to socialise from having a few drinks and laughs!

3

THE SENIOR LIST, WIND, AND WISDOM

IN THE run-up to the start of the 1984/85 season I was given a few friendly fixtures between some Highland League and Scottish League clubs, such as Elgin City v Albion Rovers, Rothes v Cowdenbeath and Forres Mechanics v Partick Thistle. This was a great way of preparing me for the new season ahead.

My very first Highland League appointment was at Lossiemouth where the home side took on Clachnacuddin from Inverness. It wasn't a particularly difficult game to handle and the away side ran out comfortable 4-1 winners. With no major talking points or controversies taking place, I was just pleased to get the match under my belt.

I took my linesmen to Lossiemouth's social club for a beer after the game and was approached by a local scribe who covered all Lossie's home matches. He sarcastically said to me, 'Well, you can only improve I suppose.' To which I retorted, 'Yes, you're right I can. But what about yourself?'

He smiled and retreated, respecting my cheeky response, I thought, as I got on fine with him after that.

My debut as a linesman in the Scottish League came a few weeks later at Forfar Athletic v St Johnstone. The match referee was George Smith from Edinburgh, one of Scotland's top officials on the FIFA list, and running the other line was Sandy Harper from Aberdeen. I was quite excited about the game as my dad was in the stand, but strangely enough, I was quite calm and not nervous at all.

At training on the Tuesday beforehand I asked Sandy Roy if there was anything I needed to know about George which might help me on the day. I was told that he would treat me well and be mindful that it was my first game and help me all he could. There was one minor detail he informed me of: that, generally, George would wear white laces on his boots and it might be a good idea if I did the same.

On arrival at the ground I found George to be very professional and he calmed any nerves I had with his quiet and calm disposition. However, when it came to getting changed into our kit, I noticed that his boots had black laces and so did Sandy Harper's! I immediately thought to myself that Big Sandy had been at the wind-up and set me up for an embarrassing situation on my first senior game. I did have black laces with me and asked George if I should change them. I am certain he was aware that I had been set up and he calmly told me it would make no difference at all.

To this day Big Sandy swears he gave me good information based on his previous encounters with George. I still have my suspicions.

The game ended up 4-0 to Forfar and there were no major issues during the 90 minutes. My journey on the Senior List had begun.

* * *

No matter what you do in life, everyone needs a guiding hand. We all require that someone who has the experience that you have not yet gained, who can give you sound advice, the motivation to succeed and the most important thing, in my opinion, is that you would trust them with your life. During my refereeing career (and other aspects of life as well!) that man was a certain A.M. Roy (previously of Elgin and now

Westhill, Aberdeen), otherwise known in the game as 'Big Honest Sandy'.

When I joined the North of Scotland Referees' Association in August 1979 Sandy was an SFA Class 2 referee, taking charge of reserve fixtures from the SPL down to Highland League and other lower grades. The welcome I got from the Big Man was warm and genuine so I took to him immediately. It was the beginning of a friendship which still lasts to this day along with his lovely wife Alison.

When you were going through the training course, which lasted from September until the entrance exam in December, you were allowed to cut your teeth in school matches and local Sunday football. My first 'big' match was out at Burghead, nine miles from my home in Elgin, in the Elgin & District Sunday Amateur League, where the local Anchors were taking on New Elgin Cosmos, and Sandy was in attendance to see how I got on.

Well, what a baptism! There were no goal nets, most of the players had a few pints inside them and were intent on kicking lumps out of each other, and one very nervous J.A. Gunn was wondering what the hell he had let himself in for! The score was 10-1 to the home side. I gave a goal that apparently I should not have given, disallowed one which should have stood, made countless other contentious decisions, ordered off two players for fighting – Robbie Nicol of Cosmos (who was the manager of New Elgin Juniors) and Watson Ralph of Anchors (a giant, hairy-arsed fisherman) – and by the end I did not know whether my arse was punch-bored or countersunk! I was of the opinion that I had an absolute disaster and began to doubt my ability to do the job.

In Sunday football then there wasn't the luxury of changing rooms and showers; you had to drive to the venue stripped for action. So, at the end of the game, I headed for my car to pull on my tracksuit and head home. Mr Roy was standing there waiting for me with, what I perceived to be, a wry smile on his face.

I was all prepared to let rip to Sandy how bad I had been and would never make a referee, etc, etc. He must have seen it in my eyes as I approached him and he said, 'Well done, John, that couldn't have been easy for you.' I took it he meant well done just for turning up!

However, the Big Man talked me through the game, pointing out mistakes and why I had made them, encouraging me about the good things he had seen and I had to realise it was, after all, my first game and things would improve the more experience I got. He calmed me right down and left me feeling a lot better about myself than I had been 15 minutes earlier. I never forgot his words of wisdom at a very tender stage in my career and there were many more to come over the coming years – along with some bollockings as well!

A couple of years later Sandy Roy was promoted to Class 1 and went on to have a very successful 17-year career at that level, culminating in running the line at the 1997 Scottish Cup Final between Kilmarnock and Falkirk, before retiring due to the SFA age limits on referees at that time. He then went on to become an SFA referee supervisor and manager of the Aberdeen & District Referees' Association, a position he still holds at the time of this book being published.

One amusing incident I recall involving Sandy and myself occurred at Tannadice in 1986 where United were at home to Clydebank. Sandy had the whistle as I ran the line in front of the main terracing. When on duty there, two very good friends of mine, Ian Ramsay and Jimmy Robb, always stood somewhere along that line behind me to watch my every move and give me a bit of stick. It was all good banter. Sandy had picked me up in his car to give me a lift down to Dundee, but

I was to get the train home after sharing a few beers with Ian and Jimmy.

When we came out for the second half, I ran across to take up my position when Ian gave me a shout that he needed to have a word with me. The upshot was that we were not going to be meeting up at our usual watering hole and had to decide where I was to see them. We arranged to meet in the Three Barrels on the Hilltown, not far from the ground. When I turned round to face the field, Big Sandy was standing in the centre circle with his arms folded, glowering across at me as if to say, 'We will get the second half under way just when you have finished organising your social arrangements, Mr Gunn!' Oops, in the bad books again.

* * *

One wintry Saturday morning I received a phone call from John Grant, then secretary of the Highland League, asking me to do a pitch inspection at Peterhead for that afternoon's match against Deveronvale which I was due to referee.

There had been overnight snow and the home club just wanted to make sure everything was going to be okay.

Outside my home in Portlethen, on the outskirts of Aberdeen, there was quite a lot of snow lying, so it seemed sensible to make the drive up to the 'Blue Toon' (so called because it always seemed to be absolutely bitter cold to every outsider who visited the place!).

On the way up the road the snow was rapidly disappearing from the ground and on my arrival at Peterhead's previous abode, Victoria Park, the pitch was green and soft – perfectly playable.

However, as I was standing in the centre circle with the respective secretaries at the time, Bill Campbell of Peterhead and Stuart McPherson of Deveronvale, there was a howling, bitterly cold, biting wind blowing right down the pitch. To play a game of football in these conditions would have been an absolute farce. As Bill, Stuart and I were discussing the possibility of players getting hypothermia and the like and trying to think of a plausible reason for a postponement, a huge gust of wind got up and caught the corrugated iron roof of the main stand, causing it to rattle furiously.

'Good God,' I said to the two officials, 'if that roof were to blow off it could cause serious injury to either spectators, players or both.' Bill and Stuart looked at one another and replied in unison, 'You are absolutely

right Mr Gunn and we will both back you all the way.'
Game off – everybody happy!

Just one more thing to do before I left for home
was to use Bill's office phone to give Tannadice a call
to book my ticket for that afternoon's game against
Celtic. Good day as it turned out – United won 2-1.

* * *

I was in the fortunate position to work as a linesman
with some of the best referees in the country, one
of them being in the top two, Brian McGinlay. In
my first season on the SFA Official List of Referees
I ran the line to Brian at Gayfield Park, home of
Arbroath FC, against Stranraer from the south-west
of Scotland.

When I started out as a linesman, I would always
keep my eyes trained on the second-last defender
and use my ear to hear the ping of the ball being
played forward.

On this occasion it did not quite work out. I was
looking across the pitch and the lone Arbroath forward
on the far side was keeping a very tight line. I was
concentrating intently on the guy – he's on, he's off,
he's on, he's off, PING – I immediately raised my
flag for offside only to see the 30-yard strike from

an Arbroath midfielder bullet into the postage stamp corner of the net. Oh shit!

Once your flag is up you have to keep it there until the referee comes over to have a word if he wishes. Brian waved away the players with an opinion on the situation and sauntered across to me. As I realised, the player I flagged for offside was in no way interfering with play and I knew that Brian was going to over-rule me and give a goal. More importantly, he knew that I knew he was giving a goal and the conversation went like this:

BM, 'How's it going today big man?'

Me, 'No bad, Brian, been better.'

BM, 'Going for a beer after the game?'

Me, 'Aye, you better believe it.'

BM, 'Lager, isn't it?'

Me, 'That'll do nicely. Oh and by the way the other linesman never goes for a drink after the game, so I will have his. Rum and coke for me.'

BM, 'No problem. Halfway line?'

And I immediately sprinted to the halfway line as a linesman does when the referee signals for a goal and he concurs with the referee's decision. Classic man management from Brian.

4

THE MILLIONAIRE TEA BOY

EVERY FOOTBALL team has a few stalwarts who have served their club with great distinction over a period of many years. Aberdeen were no different and had three such individuals who played their part in the Pittodrie club's history: Dick Donald, Chris Anderson and Teddy Scott.

Dick was one of four brothers whose father ran a dancing academy in the Granite City. The family business soon expanded into owning several cinemas and the famous His Majesty's Theatre, among other establishments, and were regarded as being the wealthiest family in the area.

Dick also played football professionally for his home-town club and Dunfermline Athletic, turning out in a handful of first-team matches. However, it was as an administrator that he really made his name, joining the Pittodrie board in 1949, being appointed vice-chairman in 1960 and eventually becoming chairman in 1970 until his death in 1993 – an amazing period of 44 years.

Despite his riches, Mr Donald was renowned for his frugal ways and every penny was regarded as a prisoner, which is probably the reason why he amassed such a fortune. One story I was told by a postman acquaintance of mine which, if true, sums the man up.

The postie was delivering a parcel to the Donald residence in the leafy suburb of Rubislaw Den and had to ring the doorbell for someone to come and collect it. Dick himself appeared at the door, greeted the postman with his cheery disposition and, as he was signing for the package, happened to look down at the man's feet. The sole of one of his boots was flapping away and clearly just about to come off, when Dick went into his pocket and produced a wedge of banknotes held together by an elastic band. The guy's eyes lit up with glee, thinking he was getting some money to buy some new footwear, when Dick took the elastic band holding the notes together, handed it to the postie and said, 'Put that round the front of your boot and it will see you out for the rest of the day laddie.'

On a personal note I found Dick Donald to be an absolute gentleman. One Saturday afternoon in the mid-1980s I was a linesman for a reserve match at Pittodrie between Aberdeen and Celtic. In those days if the first teams were playing, reserve matches took place on the same day at the opposite venue.

As usual, I arrived at the ground early. I have always been a stickler for time-keeping and to this day I can't tolerate people who are late for an appointment. As I was walking along the corridor to the referees' room, who was walking towards me but Mr Donald. He greeted me with a friendly 'Good afternoon, sir,' as he doffed his soft hat. 'I don't think we've met before. My name is Dick Donald, I am the chairman of this football club.' By that time he was in his mid-70s and didn't travel long distances to away matches. After I had introduced myself, he pointed to the tearoom and said, 'Go put your kit bag in your dressing room and I'll make you a cup of tea.' I couldn't believe what was happening, here was a man who owned half of the city of Aberdeen, calling me sir and making me a brew! What a toff.

Chris Anderson also played for the Dons for five years from 1948 before going down to Arbroath. His career was cut short after suffering a series of injuries but he stayed at Gayfield as assistant manager and in 1959 took them up to the old First Division as team boss.

Chris joined the board of Aberdeen in 1967 and three years later became vice-chairman, replacing Dick Donald who was now at the helm. He was regarded as one of the most forward-thinking and innovative administrators in the game and was the driving force behind Pittodrie becoming the first all-seated stadium in the UK. As a board member, Chris was responsible for the appointment of Alex Ferguson in 1978 which was to be the beginning of the club's most successful period in their history.

Sadly, Mr Anderson died in 1986 from the cruel debilitating illness of motor neurone disease at the age of 60. In his memory, the sports complex just up the road from Pittodrie was renamed from Linksfield to the Chris Anderson Stadium in his honour.

Teddy Scott, quite simply, was an Aberdeen legend. The man gave almost 50 years' service to the club as a player, trainer, coach, kit man and anything else he could turn his hand to.

After winning a Scottish Junior Cup winners' medal with Sunnybank in 1954, he was snapped up by Dons manager Dave Halliday. There was a lot of competition for places in the team at that time and Teddy only made one first-team appearance before moving on to spells with Brechin and Elgin City.

When his playing days were over, Teddy returned to Pittodrie to take up a training/coaching role, mainly with the reserve and youth teams. He was highly regarded by top players who came through the ranks as a mentor and father figure. His duties were wide and varied and it was well known by the Aberdeen faithful that Teddy was the first man into his work in the morning and the last one to leave at night. He dedicated his whole life to the football club.

One funny story regarding Teddy was when the Dons were playing an away tie in Europe and he had packed the wrong colour of shorts. Manager Alex Ferguson went ballistic and bawled out in front of all the players in the dressing room that he was going to give Scott the sack. Gordon Strachan, quick as a flash, then piped up, 'Aye boss, but where are you going to get the ten men to replace him!' Needless to say Teddy kept his job.

I came into contact with Teddy on numerous occasions as a referee. When I was working shifts for a printing company in Aberdeen, he would often ask me to referee bounce games on midweek afternoons for the youngsters at the club. Colleague Mike Pocock, who worked shifts in the fish industry, and I took it in turn to help Teddy out. These were fantastic experiences as quite often there would be the odd first-team player taking part working their way back from injury or suspension.

Teddy was also an absolute gem of a man and after every match I would be invited into his office (a youth team coach having his own room – that's how highly thought of he was) for a cup of tea and sometimes a dram. His office was stacked full of football memorabilia – programmes, pennants, photographs, tops, trophies, etc – you name it, Teddy had it. I thoroughly enjoyed the chats we had either reminiscing about days gone by or serious issues happening within the game at that time.

The highest accolade Aberdeen paid Teddy was by awarding him a testimonial match in 1999. Alex Ferguson took up a full-strength Manchester United team to take on the Dons. The game was a sell-out and their biggest crowd for years, such was the affection and regard the Aberdeen public had for the man.

In 2013, after Teddy's passing the previous year, the Europa Suite at the stadium was renamed the

Teddy Scott Lounge and redecorated to commemorate his contribution to the club. Another proper gentleman gone.

5

BLUNDERS, BANTER, AND DOCTOR DEATH

BUCKIE THISTLE versus Fraserburgh was usually quite an enthralling Highland League fixture to referee with plenty of goals to keep the fans happy. But there was one in the late 1980s which I remember for all the wrong reasons.

Midway through the first half a hopeful ball from Fraserburgh was punted high and deep into the Buckie half. Their centre-half Donald Buchanan totally misjudged its flight and Fraserburgh centre-forward Dave Robertson took full advantage and volleyed his shot over the goalkeeper.

It was heading for the net when I turned towards the halfway line to signal the goal. Now, when a referee signals for a goal, the linesman on that side, if he agrees, should sprint to the halfway line also. The man in question, Alastair Boyne from Lhanbryde, did nothing. He didn't go to the halfway line or flag for offside or an infringement, but just stood opposite the six-yard box looking across the park. I tried to attract his attention by gesturing to him to give me a clue as to what he was doing. As there was no response I was compelled to go over to him and ask what the problem was. 'It's not a goal,' he said, 'the ball went past the post.' Somewhat bemused, I asked him if he was absolutely sure. He was adamant it went past the post, so I awarded a goal kick which was taken extremely quickly by the Buckie custodian Alex Innes. At that point I said to myself, 'What the hell are you playing at? You know that was a bloody goal!' However, once the ball was back in play there was no way I could reverse the decision.

What actually happened was it had been a rising shot which hit the junction of the net with the stanchion at such a pace, forcing one of the pins which held it into the ground to pop out. The ball whizzed down the net, through the gap because of the missing pin, hit an advertising board at the back of the goal and ended up on the other side of the goalpost. This, of course, all happened in a split second and this information came at half-time from the other linesman, Alan Birch, who was positioned on the halfway line at the other side of the field and had a perfect view of the incident. In those days it was frowned upon for him to intervene. I wish he had as I would have taken his word over Alistair Boyne any day of the week and it would have saved me a great deal of hassle.

Ultimately the decision was mine and I took full responsibility for this ghastly error, but how on earth Alastair thought the ball went past the post is beyond belief. The mistake I made was turning away before the ball hit the net. Believe me, it never happened again!

Fraserburgh eventually won the game 1-0 much to their delight – and my relief.

* * *

I have had the privilege of working as a linesman with some of the best referees in the business. Unfortunately, there were exceptions, not necessarily in ability but more in their attitude and treatment of their fellow officials.

One such individual was a pathologist from Edinburgh, Andrew Waddell, aka 'Dr Death' because of his chosen profession.

I was appointed to run the line at a Dundee United v Hearts Premier League match in 1990 with the bold doctor as referee. As you will know by now, I am a Dundee United fan but when on duty I was there to do a job to the best of my ability. Incidentally, the other linesman was colleague and good friend Larry Officer, a lifelong Hearts fan. Perhaps Maureen Cooper, who handled the referee appointments for the Scottish Football League, was trying to even things up.

Anyway, despite linesmen being given an instruction sheet by the Scottish Football Association at the start of every season, Dr Death had his own instructions. Without going into detail, it was you must do this, you must do that, don't do this, don't do that. In his little world he knew better.

As United and Hearts were two of the top clubs in the league, this was always a keenly contested encounter with no quarter being asked or given. The game started off quite evenly with no real controversy then Hearts scored late in the first half.

Midway through the second half, the game exploded into life as the Jambos' centre-forward Wayne Foster was upended just outside the penalty area by Maurice Malpas. Foster was furious and jumped up to confront Malpas and an almighty melee ensued with quite a few of the players gesticulating, pushing and jostling with one another. Maurice had the presence of mind to walk away from the incident to retreat into his own six-yard box. When order had been restored you could sense the referee was looking for the culprit who had committed the foul to issue a yellow, or even red, card. He had either forgotten or had no idea who it was. Instead of going over to consult with Larry, who would have been able to identify Malpas as the incident happened right in front of him, he chose to just ignore it. It looked to me as if he didn't trust Larry to do his job. Arrogance personified.

United were now pushing forward for an equaliser and had quite a lot of the forward play. With around ten minutes left they were attacking down the left and the ball was crossed into the box. It looked as if it had been slightly over-hit as the intended tangerine-shirted targets could not get on the end of the delivery. However, Ray McKinnon, United's talented young midfielder, had other ideas. He chased the bouncing ball along the goal line and attempted to hitch-kick it back into the goalmouth with Hearts' keeper Henry Smith just behind him. Ray slipped in his attempt to play the ball and ended up on his backside. Suddenly, the referee's whistle went and Waddell pointed to the penalty spot. I could not believe what I had seen.

Most referees in those days, when they gave a penalty, pointed to the spot then ran to the goal line and turned round. The train of thought was that by doing so all the players would be in front of you which made any protests easier to handle. Not the bold Waddell, who marched up to – and stood on – the penalty spot, allowed the Hearts players to surround him with their complaints and then gestured with his arm towards yours truly.

I didn't think anything of it at the time and United scored from the penalty to make the final result 1-1. As the three of us were coming off the park at full time I was subjected to some of the most vile abuse from several Hearts players, particularly Smith. I asked Waddell if he was going to do anything about it and he just looked in front of him and said to me, 'Just get inside.' I was not a happy bunny!

In the referees' dressing room at Tannadice there were two baths and one shower. Waddell and Larry opted for the baths and I went for a shower. As the adrenalin was now beginning to subside within me, I suddenly realised why I got all that abuse at full time. When Waddell had gestured across to me with his arm he had told the Hearts players that it was me who gave the decision for a penalty! I shouted 'you bastard' and came out of the shower to remonstrate with him.

Thankfully, Larry, who had been anticipating this response, jumped up quickly and managed to put his hand across my chest to prevent me from landing a right hook on Waddell's chin. I had my say on the matter, dried myself and was out of that dressing room within a minute and off to the pub to see some of my Dundee pals to calm down.

In my opinion Waddell was a decent referee; in fact he was on the FIFA list. As a person he let himself, and me, down very badly in what I can only describe as a spineless and despicable act. I telephoned Maureen Cooper at the Scottish Football League on the Monday morning to ask if it would be possible to never work with Dr Death again. I was accommodated in my desire, thankfully.

* * *

One of the biggest laughs I had during my refereeing career was at the expense of a guy who became a good friend of mine, the former Aberdeen, Dundee United and Motherwell man John Gardiner. John lived round the corner from me in Portlethen and was then keeping goal for Huntly in the Highland League.

The game in question was a Highland League fixture at Christie Park, Huntly, against Inverness Thistle.

It was a very even, keenly contested encounter when the Jags opened the scoring midway through the first half. Play continued in the same vein during the second half until late on when Huntly really put the pressure on to press for an equaliser. With two minutes left on the clock Huntly earned a corner with most of their players in and around the Inverness penalty area. When the ball came over it was easily collected by their keeper, Jim Calder, who spotted his team-mate Fraser Taylor standing on his own on the halfway line and immediately booted the ball up the park.

It was sailing deep into the Huntly half with Taylor in hot pursuit but the chances of getting to the ball first were 60/40 in big John's favour. Taylor had a bit of a nasty streak in him and, as the Huntly custodian came out to the edge of his box to receive the ball, he slid in with his studs up. John saw it coming, gathered the ball in his hands and easily side-stepped the challenge. As there was only just over a minute left, I waved for the keeper to play on as he had possession of the ball and could play it up the park for his team-mates to chase that elusive goal.

Big John had other ideas. He was so incensed with Taylor's challenge he put the ball on the ground and remonstrated by waving and pointing his finger at him with a few choice words as well. Fraser Taylor just smiled at him with a look that said, 'Oh really?' and toe-poked the ball into the empty net. The big man was furious, but there was nothing I could do about it because I had waved to play on as he had an advantage with the ball in his hands. What a numpty! To this day he still maintains that he did not hear me shouting to play on. Aye, right!

The manager of Huntly at the time was legendary Aberdeen striker Joe Harper. He was standing at the bar of the Huntly Social Club when I walked in to order a beer for myself and two linesmen. When Big John came in he made a beeline for me, but was stopped in his tracks by his boss who bellowed at him, 'Don't you dare have a go at the referee, he was right and you were wrong. If I had a dunce's cap handy I would make you wear it and stand you in the corner until the bus is ready to leave for Aberdeen, you plonker!' Enough said.

As I said earlier, I became good friends with John and was actually on his testimonial committee after he served ten years at Huntly.

* * *

Brechin, the lovely, picturesque Angus town, houses probably the friendliest football club in the world. Brechin City have always been a very well-run organisation with their most well-known former chairman David Will being a past president of the SFA and a senior vice president of FIFA, along with other colleagues down the years such as George Johnston, Davie Birse, Ken Ferguson and many others, always keeping the club in the black within the lower echelons of the Scottish game.

I have very fond memories of my appointments as a linesman at Glebe Park. The hospitality after the match was legendary and no official ever wanted to drive there as not to partake would have been very rude indeed! In fact, it has been rumoured that some well-known west coast referees spent a Saturday night in Brechin after officiating there, courtesy of the aforementioned George Johnston.

One of many funny incidents at the Glebe springs immediately to mind as I make my journey down memory lane. City were playing Falkirk and I was running the line at the 'Hedge' side of the ground. Glebe Park is very tight and if a spectator was leaning on the railing he could actually reach over and tap the linesman on the shoulder. Anyway, there was a group of young lads, who had sampled some of the refreshments at the local hostelries, and they were intent on giving yours truly a hard time. It really was just good-natured banter which didn't affect me at all.

However, as always, there is one guy who has to be the loudest and he kept ranting on about me being an absolute 'arsehole' throughout the game. Midway into the second half there was a stoppage in play due to an injury at the other end of the park and the guy was still giving me GBH of the earhole. So I turned round to him and said, 'Listen pal, you paid money to watch me today so who's the arsehole?!' His mates fell about laughing, took the absolute piss out of him and he was never heard again.

These days you would get sacked by the authorities for doing something like that.

Portlethen was once a quaint little fishing village, but because of the upsurge in the oil industry, by the time I moved there in 1985 it had become a small town with a population of around 5,000. It was very cosmopolitan as families moved north from Glasgow, Ayrshire, Edinburgh, Fife, England and abroad, to seek their fortune from the 'black gold'.

Because most were 'incomers' they all tended to get on well together, but the minority locals were suspicious of the 'white settlers' who had come up, as they saw it, to take all their jobs. As the vast majority came from the west of Scotland, their football team was usually either Celtic or Rangers.

Being a referee, I was naturally given a fair bit of stick, but these guys were real football fans and the banter on the streets and in the local pubs was great fun. In the 25 years I lived there I made a lot of good friends, which I still have to this day, before moving into the city itself.

Every year the local residents raised money for the senior citizens of the town to have a big Christmas party. In August 1987, it was decided by the Celtic and Rangers supporters to have a fundraising sports day which would include a football match on the Sunday morning, followed by darts, dominoes and pool competitions in the local Leathan Arms for the rest of the day. My good mate, Celtic fan Alex McMillan, asked me if I would referee the game, but there would be a slight difference from normal circumstances. Instead of receiving a match fee, I had to pay £5 for the privilege, which was the same as all the players. I quickly agreed, as it was for a good cause, and there I was, ready to officiate at my first 'Old Firm' clash.

On the day before the sports day, I was a linesman at a Dundee v St Mirren match at Dens Park. I think I was more nervous about refereeing the charity encounter the following day. However, I needn't have worried as it was played in a good spirit and ended up being a good laugh.

The Celtic lads had a much younger team and ended up winning 7-1. With the score at 6-0, Rangers got a corner and for a joke I said to the Celtic centre-half Bob Hudson, 'If this ball comes anywhere near me I am going to melt it into the top corner.' 'Aye, right,' said Bob. When the corner was taken, I was standing a few yards behind him as the ball skimmed off his head and fell perfectly for me to volley a shot for goal. The keeper was well beaten, and the ball was, indeed, heading for the top corner when Jimmy Nugent jumped up and palmed it over the bar. To the consternation of wee Jim, I awarded a penalty and yellow-carded him for deliberately handling the ball! Ralph Ballantyne then proceeded to balloon his spot-kick over the bar. It was all in good fun and over £1,000 was raised that day for the pensioners' Christmas shindig. I had got through my first, and only, Celtic v Rangers encounter unscathed.

I was quite friendly with the Celtic contingent in Portlethen, and it was well known by all that I was a Dundee United fan. When the Tangerines reached the Scottish Cup Final in 1988, I was asked if I wanted a lift to the game on the Aberdeen-based Grampian Emerald Supporters' Club coach. As long as I could get my own ticket there would be plenty of room for me. I accepted their kind offer and had a good day out, apart from a 2-1 defeat, as the Hoops completed the double in their centenary year.

The following August I was appointed to run the line at Tannadice for the visit of the champions. This led to much hilarity and banter in the local pub, where I was accused of going to 'fix' the match in the home side's favour! It did turn out to be a 1-0 victory for United, but due to a horrendous back-pass from Mick McCarthy to let Kevin Gallagher in to score, more than any favouritism on my part.

A few of the Leathan Arms's local customers had attended the game, including Frankie Clark, Billy Wood and Dite Alexander. They presented me with a trophy that evening containing the inscription 'To the Most Baised Linesman in Scotland'. You will note that the spelling of the word 'biased' is incorrect. It turned out the lads had the trophy inscribed on a recent trip to Ireland and hadn't noticed the mistake, which led to even more hilarity.

Another occasion I remember taking stick from fans was at a testimonial match in Peterhead in honour of their long-serving centre-half Ally Buchan. Supplying the opposition was none other than Dundee United. I ran the line in front of where a fair number of Arabs had congregated, who included friends of mine, Shuggy Falconer, Davie Bowman, Gary Melville and others. They had clearly had a few beers prior to kick-off and throughout the game proceeded to give me a fair bit of stick. United's midfield hard man, Dave 'Psycho' Bowman, was about to take a throw-in alongside me and had heard what was going on. He pleaded with them to give me a break as I was only doing my job, but when he was told I was their mate, he turned to me and said, 'Christ, big man, with mates like that, you certainly don't need any enemies.'

6

SPIES, EUROPE, AND POLITICS

THE SIGHT of an SFA referee supervisor in attendance at one of your games was quite often a reason to change from your normal style of refereeing to one HE wanted to see. There were always edicts coming out from the SFA offices which these guys liked to see implemented or they would not give you a good mark in their report to the governing body.

Don't get me wrong, the supervisors were necessary to monitor referees' performances and to earmark potential candidates for promotion to a higher level. However, it was really frustrating when they got it 100 per cent wrong, perhaps denying officials a good report or even a step up.

During my time as a referee and linesman I have no real axe to grind. I went up through the grades from schoolboys, juveniles, amateurs, juniors and ultimately on to the SFA Official List in 1984. I know I was quite well thought of in the lower levels, particularly in the North Region Junior Leagues where I refereed every major cup final in the area. Despite never getting above Grade 3A I thoroughly enjoyed my time and met many good people, and some real characters as well, and when I retired from the Senior List in the early 1990s it was due to pressing work commitments rather than moaning about bad reports or thinking I was better than someone else who did get promoted. And believe me, there were quite a few who did!

One such injustice for me from a supervisor occurred at a Scottish Junior Cup tie between Carnoustie Panmure and Renfrew from the west coast in 1988. Junior cup ties were always fiercely competitive and it was not unusual to issue at least six yellow cards and a couple of reds. This was no exception. It was a very close encounter when Renfrew went into the half-time interval with a 1-0 lead which ended up being the final score.

The supervisor, a guy from Dundee called Wilkie if I remember correctly, should have gone to Specsavers before travelling the short distance up the coast to Carnoustie! He was standing near to the halfway line when the Renfrew centre-back intentionally tripped a Panmure forward as he was approaching the penalty area. The Carnoustie player got up immediately and spat in the Renfrew man's face. I booked the defender for the foul and rightly sent off the attacker. The Carnoustie bench and committee men were furious but clearly did not see the incident properly.

When I was leaving the field at the end of the game the Carnoustie secretary, a giant of a man, gave me a right mouthful, making his feelings on the red card known to everyone who was still in the ground but without uttering any offensive language towards me. I ignored it and carried on to my dressing room.

After having my shower and getting dressed there was a knock on the dressing room door. It was the big Carnoustie secretary, with a rather sheepish look on his face, and he asked if he could come in. No problem. 'I have just come from our dressing room,' he mumbled, 'and the player you sent off has admitted to everyone that he did spit at his opponent and apologised to his team-mates for letting them down. I am here to apologise to you for the way I shouted at you at the end of the match. You had a good game and that decision was obviously correct but I didn't see it.' He held out his hand as an offer of apology, which I accepted of course, and he invited me into their social club to buy me a beer. I didn't need to be asked twice!

Where exactly does the supervisor fit in to all this? If he didn't see the incident clearly, then why did he not approach me after the game and ask me the reason why I sent the player off? Instead he chose to give me a moderate report, stating I had wrongly red-carded the Carnoustie forward. How the hell would he know if he didn't ask?

I was absolutely incensed with Mr Wilkie. I could have appealed against the report, but it was widely considered to be a waste of time for rookie referees like myself, and I was advised to take it on the chin.

Another occasion I had reason to question the wisdom of a supervisor was after a game at Huntly where they were hosts to Inverness Caledonian. The man in question was one of the local guys from my association, Aberdeen & District, called Robbie Harrold. The same Robbie Harrold who had taken the classes in Elgin a few years ago.

It was one of those games when you just knew that everything had gone well. It was quite an exciting fixture also, with Inverness racing to a three-goal half-time lead and Huntly coming roaring back in the second half to earn a 3-3 draw. I dished out only one yellow card during the match, to Inverness skipper Peter Corbett, who was getting on a bit and had lost what little pace he had, for a deliberate trip. I really enjoyed the 90 minutes and felt good about my performance as there had been no major issues at all.

At training on the Tuesday after, Robbie took me aside to discuss the game and he told me that he thought I had done very well and was always in control, letting the play flow when I could. My mark was to be 85 per cent which I was happy about. There were always a couple of small negatives, even with a good performance, and he chose to question my positioning at certain times. Then Robbie hit me with a totally unexpected question. 'Don't you think you fraternise with the players too much?' Now, I am fairly well educated and know what the word 'fraternise' means. I thought about it for a couple of seconds and replied, 'Do you mean you think I talk to the players too much?' Robbie replied that, yes, I was perhaps too familiar with them. I then said, 'Hang on a minute, didn't you say at the start of the conversation that I was in total control of the game?' He replied in the affirmative to which I hastily and quite abruptly said to him, 'The reason I was in total control of the game WAS because I talked to the players throughout, what on earth are you looking for?'

He couldn't give me an answer as there wasn't one.

I firmly believe that as a football referee you have to man-manage players in such a way that you treat them with respect as well as dishing out the discipline as and when required. If the authorities were looking for something different then I was in the wrong game. It certainly made me think about where football was heading with regards to relationships between players and referees.

* * *

When a referee makes the SFA Official List there are three main ambitions he would like to achieve: promotion to a higher grade, a major cup final and at least one appointment to either a European club competition tie or an international match. In my case it was the European trip.

In September 1987 I was absolutely delighted to be appointed as a linesman to the European Cup first round second leg in East Germany between Dynamo Berlin and Bordeaux. The referee would be my ex-work colleague and friend Bob Valentine from Dundee with the other flag being carried by Derek Miller of Garrowhill. Bob was regarded as one of the best referees, not just in Scotland, but the world over and it was always a pleasure to work with him and share his company off the park also. He was the other one of the top two referees that I had worked with.

In those days there was no fourth official from a neutral country, this appointment being taken up by a referee from the home nation. There was no match fee as such as the payment you received was for 'out-of-pocket expenses' as you had to take three days off work to make the trip. We were all given the same amount which was paid in cash in Swiss francs and amounted to the equivalent of £210 (£70 per day). A tidy wee sum back then considering I took a week's holiday and therefore did not have any loss of earnings. I would really like to know what our present-day officials are picking up for their efforts now.

This was my first visit to a communist country as this was two years before the Berlin Wall came down and the ultimate unification of the two German nations. It was a very weird experience as it was like going back in time. The East was way behind the West in terms of technology, transport, fashion, etc. The industrial buildings reminded me of the UK in the

1960s with large, smoking chimneys dominating the landscape.

Bordeaux, who were captained by the classy French international midfielder Jean Tigana, led 2-0 from the first leg and knew they would be in for a tough game as Dynamo had just won nine consecutive league championships and were notoriously difficult to beat on their own patch.

The match itself was largely uneventful with the away side securing a comfortable 2-0 victory to go through to the next round 4-0 on aggregate.

After the match we were treated to a slap-up meal and drinks by our hosts, ex-FIFA referee Heinz Einbeck and an interpreter whose name escapes me. They were with us throughout our time in Berlin, meeting us off the plane, taking us for meals, trips round the city and generally making us feel relaxed and welcome in unfamiliar surroundings.

The whole experience was most enjoyable and one I will cherish for the rest of my life.

* * *

If there was one aspect I hated about the refereeing movement it was the politics. Guys who thought they were better than others making sure they talked to the correct people in the corridors of power, some back-stabbing colleagues in order to further their own careers, keeping close to their supervisors and befriending senior referees in other parts of the country in a bid to get them to influence their supervisors.

I was not naïve I knew you had to keep your nose clean to have any chance of advancement but the antics of some were absolutely pathetic. I preferred to do my talking on the pitch and only confided in people I really trusted, who would give me honesty and not bullshit.

The Aberdeen & District Referees' Association, in line with all others in Scotland, met every month throughout the season to discuss local and national refereeing topics. Regularly, we would invite someone from within football to be our guest speaker for the evening.

On one occasion the then secretary of the SFA, Ernie Walker, was invited to address the association in his last season in office. Ernie was affectionately known in some football circles as 'The Ayatollah' because of his hard-line approach to certain aspects of the game, particularly discipline. In my opinion, Ernie was a genuine football man and an excellent administrator and, despite his critics, I believe that not one person who followed in his footsteps as secretary or chief executive of the SFA have come anywhere close to his passion and expertise.

Ernie gave quite an informative and humorous speech which was followed by a short question-and-answer session. Davie Argo, a long-serving amateur referee who was not the sharpest tool in the box, had a question which caused Ernie to blow a gasket and embarrassment among the members present.

Davie asked, 'Why do Celtic and Rangers never seem to get drawn together in the semi-finals of both domestic cup competitions?' The implication from Davie was that, somehow, the draw was rigged so that the Old Firm could meet in the final.

Ernie was furious and you could see him lean over to then secretary Bill Crichton, clearly asking for the identity of this individual. Davie was never in a position to progress any higher than amateur level, but if he had been it would have ended that Monday evening. That was the way it worked and was perhaps why Davie asked the question in the first place.

At one annual general meeting I was given a lift into Aberdeen by colleague Alan Freeland who also lived in Portlethen. Alan was the supreme politician. We actually went on the SFA Senior List on the same day, but he went on to bigger and better things because of who he knew. I have no personal axe to grind with Alan, but my main gripe was that he got promoted ahead of referees who were far better than he was. It was my firm view that the main reason Freeland reached the FIFA List of Referees to officiate at European and international level was because of the friendship he formed with George Smith on a trip to Portugal where he was a linesman. On retiring, George became a supervisor at the SFA and would most certainly have been a big influence in Alan's career progression.

Alan was regarded by fans at that time as being one of the worst referees in Scotland, along with another FIFA colleague, Mike McCurry, who must also have had friends in very high places. Controversy followed that pair every other week.

Anyway, back to the meeting. There was quite a serious topic brought up by an amateur referee on behalf of his colleagues at that level. I cannot for the life of me remember what the issue was but the guy put up an excellent case for the association's help and I spoke up very strongly in his favour, despite the fact it would be 'rocking the boat'.

As usual, it was played down by senior members of the group and it never went any further. This only cemented the belief by referees at the lower levels that the association was mainly run for the benefit of the SFA Senior List officials.

On the way home in the car, Alan questioned why I had been so supportive of the amateur referee. I replied that I had totally agreed with his argument and we did live in a democracy after all. He then suggested that in future I should perhaps not be so vociferous at meetings, clearly inferring that it may harm my future prospects.

As we approached my house to be dropped off, I said to Alan quite strongly, 'When I get up in the morning and go for a shave, I can look myself in the mirror. Can you do the same?' Our relationship has been, at best, tepid ever since.

7

HIGHLAND LEAGUE CHARACTERS

THROUGHOUT MY years in football I have met some fantastic people and made many friends. There have also been some chancers who I have crossed swords with along the way as well. As a referee I met quite a few 'characters' in my time and shared quite a few laughs and some hairy incidents with some of them. Here are a few:

George 'Dod' Stephen, a free-scoring centre-forward, started his playing career with Banks o' Dee Juniors, stepping up to the Highland League with Buckie Thistle before moving on to Peterhead. Despite being a very good player, with an eye for goal, Dod was one of the biggest moaners on a pitch and he absolutely hated referees. An example of this was when I was out for a pint one Saturday evening with another footballing friend of mine, Gordon Christie, president of Banks o' Dee. We were walking up the stairs to the Hayloft Bar in Aberdeen as Dod and some of his mates were on their way down. Dod took one look at me and said to Gordon, 'What the hell are you doing out with this arsehole, Gordon, I thought you had better taste than that.' Gordon gave him a rollicking as I continued on my way and could hear Dod laughing as he departed the premises.

It was nothing personal, Dod just did not like referees – any of them – and we all had problems with him over the years. That is until I was appointed to handle a friendly between Aberdeen and Peterhead on a winter's Wednesday night at Pittodrie, then it was payback time!

The match had been organised to give some game time to some of the Dons players who had recently been out with either injury or suspension, one of them being Alex McLeish, a future Scotland manager.

The game itself was easy to handle as it was played in the correct spirit, but two incidents did not please Mr Stephen at all. The first occurred in the first half with Peterhead attacking towards the Merkland Stand.

The ball had been played up to Dod from midfield facing his own goal. He turned round McLeish and was on the point of shooting when Big Eck stuck out a leg, bringing him down just inside the penalty box. 'Penalty, ref!' shouted Dod. I stood and smiled at him and said, 'Defender touched the ball, play on.' He was absolutely furious and was about to have a right go at me but as the ball had been gathered by the goalkeeper and cleared up the park, I turned, ran to follow play and his chance was gone.

Aberdeen had gone into a 2-0 lead and were seeing the game out comfortably when, with a few minutes to go, a cross came in from the Peterhead right-winger with Dod going up to meet the ball with his head when McLeish gave him a nudge in the back which was enough for him to misdirect his header wide. Again, the shout from Dod was, 'That's a definite penalty ref, you have got to give that one!' Once more I stood and smiled at him and said, 'Goal kick, get up and get on with it.' By this time I think he was so pissed off he couldn't be bothered to challenge the decision.

After everyone had showered and changed we were all invited into the Pittodrie boardroom for sandwiches and refreshments. I was enjoying the hospitality and a chat with my two linesmen when I was approached by Dod, who asked if he could have a quiet word. Absolutely no problem and we moved to a corner where no one could hear us.

George, in a very calm manner I have to say, asked why I hadn't given the two penalties that he described as being 'stonewallers'. I hesitated just for a moment and then with a huge smile on my face whispered to him, 'The reason why you didn't get those decisions tonight was for all the back-chat and shit my colleagues and I have taken from you throughout your career and I thought it was about time I had my turn to give you some.' A somewhat bemused Dod thanked me for my honesty and went back to his group without ever mentioning our conversation.

A short while after Dod and his family moved out to where I lived in Portlethen and we shared a pint or two in our local, the Leathan Arms. I never had any more bother with Dod on the park after that. I don't know whether it was down to our little chat at Pittodrie or whether he was just getting wiser as he got older.

Just for the record – if that match had been a competitive one with something at stake, I would have awarded the two penalties, as the score would have mattered. However, it was worth it to teach a young man a very valuable lesson!

Charlie Duncan was one of the most talented players I have ever seen play anywhere, never mind just in the Highland League. He started his career in England during the 1960s with Chelsea, also turning out for Wimbledon and Crystal Palace, before returning to Scotland with Montrose. His Highland League clubs were Inverness Thistle, Buckie Thistle, Peterhead and Fraserburgh. It is my belief that Charlie is the only player to play in the Highland League during the 1960s, '70s, '80s and '90s – a tremendous feat indeed.

But it is his time with Fraserburgh that I will remember the most as he spent over 25 years at Bellslea Park as player, player-manager and manager covering well over 1,000 games.

Charlie was a cocky, happy-go-lucky sort of guy who everyone took an instant liking to. As a player he would laugh and joke his way through games, often asking members of the crowd where free kicks and throw-ins should be taken from rather than seek the officials' advice. He was still playing for the Broch when he took over as manager in 1984, the same year I was promoted to the SFA Senior List of Referees.

I always got on well with Charlie because of his very pleasant disposition, but we did have our differences on a couple of occasions. I think it was my second season in the Highland League when Fraserburgh travelled to Allan Park to play Cove Rangers. For some strange reason Charlie seemed to be really wound up that day which was totally unlike him. He was running around like a headless chicken, diving needlessly into challenges and generally growling at everyone around him. Despite my attempts to calm him down I eventually had to give him a yellow card for a nasty tackle on an unsuspecting opponent. I had strong words with him and told him straight – any more of that and he would be off. Lo and behold, two minutes later he decked the same guy in the same manner as before and he sheepishly walked towards me to accept the inevitable red card I was about to dish out. And this was all before half-time. At the end of the game he apologised to me for his behaviour, which really had been totally out of character, and said it wouldn't happen again. Fraserburgh lost 2-1 and Charlie knew his absence from the pitch in the second half would not have helped his team's cause.

Perhaps it was just a bad day at the office for the Broch boss, we all had them. Remember THAT game between Buckie Thistle and Fraserburgh where I gave the goal that wasn't? Yes, Charlie was the manager of the Broch that day and he knew that I knew I had made a blunder of monumental proportions. To that end he didn't need to say anything to me until we were all trooping off the pitch at the end of the game when he sidled up alongside and whispered to me, 'You are no' the best referee in the Highland League and you're definitely no' the worst, but, by Christ, you're as bloody honest as the day is long!'

That will do for me, Charlie boy, that will do for me!

The last time I had a chat with Charlie was at Gayfield where Fraserburgh were taking on Arbroath in a Scottish Cup tie. Dundee United did not have a game that day and I got a lift down the road to Arbroath from an Aberdeen-based sports journalist pal of mine, Scott Burns. The match finished 0-0 and can only be remembered for one of the worst refereeing performances I have seen with TWO players ordered off and another NINE booked.

After the game I nipped to the pub across the road, The Tutties Neuk, for a quick pint to allow Scott to conduct his post-match interviews. I then went back to the ground and found Scott just as he was about to interview Charlie, who spotted me immediately. He came up to me, shook my hand, gave me a big hug and asked how I was doing, before we started having a conversation about days gone by. Scott was quite pissed off as he was trying hard to get Charlie's verdict on the game and I was severely getting in the way. Scott eventually handed me his keys and told me to bugger off back to his car so he could get on with his job. Charlie and I had a good old laugh about it and left, as always, on good terms.

Ian 'Thainer' Thain was one of the finest goalkeepers ever to have graced the Highland League. He had an absolutely outstanding career spanning 22 years with Deveronvale, Keith, Inverurie Locos and Cove Rangers. Thainer's biggest assets which stood out for me were his commitment and enthusiasm for the game he loved. The most annoying thing about the man was nobody had a bad word to say about him! He really was one of the most respected and well-liked characters within the Highland League scene.

As a referee I can honestly say that Ian never gave me any trouble at all on the pitch as he never argued with decisions given against him or his team. He would, on occasion, ask a question but after an explanation was given he would go back to his position and, being the intelligent guy he was, knew full well that any decision was not going to be reversed by any comment that he might have made.

Thainer spent 16 very successful seasons at Keith, making a club-record 616 appearances and, just to sum up how highly thought of he was, on his 50th birthday Ian was made Keith's first ever club ambassador. A fantastic accolade indeed.

Ian now does his MC stints on the north-east after-dinner circuit. I have met him at a few and he carries out his duties with his trademark enthusiasm and humour. He always has a few stories to tell about his time in the Highland League. There are some that I could not repeat in this book for fear of a visit from the local constabulary for one or both of us! One of nature's finest.

Donald Buchanan was an uncompromising centre-half, starting out at Deveronvale before spending a few seasons with Buckie Thistle and having a short spell at Cove Rangers. Donald was labelled as a 'hard man' because he rarely let opponents get past him which led to him receiving a substantial amount of yellow and red cards. It was a standing joke among the refereeing fraternity that if Buchanan was playing you would write his name in the book before the start of the match and just fill in the time when the inevitable occurred.

The big man moved to Portlethen with his family after I had finished refereeing at senior level and, as with George Stephen, I shared a few beers with him in my local. Despite his reputation I always got on well with Donald, on and off the field. I just felt he was a big, honest clogger with no hidden agenda and he always treated me with respect, which was not the case with a number of my colleagues.

One trait that he did possess, however, was that he was one of the most vain people I have ever come across. He always turned up immaculate, on and off the park. With Buckie he adopted the same hairstyle as Charlie Nicholas, of Celtic and Arsenal fame, and did not like to get his kit dirty as it would spoil his image. I also have it on good authority he hated wearing a seatbelt in his car as it might crease his shirt. What a poser!

As we shared the same local pub, I became quite friendly with Donald and we reminisced about our days in the Highland League on many occasions. On one such evening we were joined by one of the regulars, a real football man called Brian Daniels, and he was quizzing Donald about his playing days and his dealings with me. 'So, you played centre-half,' Brian said to him. 'Gunner must have booked you a few times then.' The big man confirmed that had been the case on several occasions during his career. 'Did he ever send you off?' Brian enquired. Donald replied quite emphatically, 'No he did not, because when Mr Gunn said that was my last foul I knew he bloody well meant it!' I had never thought about it before, but he was right, I had never sent him off. I took his remark to be a compliment.

Eddie Copeland was another top goalscorer in the Highland League, starting his career in the seniors with Montrose but making a name for himself with Huntly when they won five back-to-back league titles during the mid-1990s. Eddie always gave 100 per cent in every game which was something I liked to see in a player. If he had a fault it was that he would get so wound up during matches and let his temper get the better of him if he got clattered by an opponent. Some referees would stand back and watch him get his retribution and then send him off for retaliation.

I liked Eddie as he was a genuinely nice guy and I took a different approach with him. When he got badly fouled in a game the first thing I did was shout to him, 'Don't even think about it, Eddie.' It seemed to stop him in his tracks as he would get up and walk away. Eddie once told me he reckoned that I had talked him out of quite a few red cards. I haven't seen him for years but I used to bump into his dad on a few occasions in Ye Olde Frigate bar in Aberdeen when I lived up there. Good guy, Eddie, another gentleman.

Willie Grant, or 'King Willie' as he was affectionately known in the north of Scotland, is probably the biggest legend in Highland League history, scoring a phenomenal 348 goals in 255 games over eight seasons for Elgin City. This was way back in the early 1960s and before my time in Elgin, but I worked alongside him at *The Northern Scot* where he was an advertising sales executive and he had some great stories to tell.

After his very successful spell at Elgin he moved to the Highland capital to be player-manager of Inverness Thistle. He was still involved in the game when I was refereeing in the juniors, back at his beloved Borough Briggs as manager of Elgin City. Ill health eventually ended a short spell there.

My family became very close to Willie and his wife Jill and we shared quite a few meals and drinks at one another's homes. As I said earlier, with his near 30-year involvement in the game, Willie had a host of tales to tell about his experiences. One of them involved a top referee.

Despite being a prolific goalscorer, finding the net with consummate ease, Willie had a very short fuse and got into a fair bit of bother with officials. After he was sent off against Buckie Thistle by Frank Phillips for dissent, Elgin decided to appeal against the decision. This meant a long train journey down to Glasgow to appear in front of the SFA Referee Committee. Frank Phillips was also on that train and Willie sat opposite him, hoping that being polite and chatty to him might help his case. At the meeting Frank did not oblige and, because of his previous record, 'King Willie' got a four-week suspension (in those days bans were served by length of time, not an amount of games). On the journey back up north Willie, although not very happy at the outcome, again sat opposite Frank and chatted away as if nothing had happened. Halfway through the trip Mr Phillips decided he would go to answer a call of nature. It was then that Willie noticed he had a brand new pair of gloves sitting on the table in front of him and proceeded to throw them out of the train window. 'That'll teach the bastard,' he thought.

Despite his on-field antics, Willie was a very gentle, placid man whose company I loved to be in. The world became a poorer place when he passed away in 2007 aged 71. In a twist of fate, he will also feature later.

Jim Blacklaw was one character I always found to be fair and easy to deal with. The Aberdonian forward went down to Leicester City as a youngster but unfortunately did not make the grade. He came back to Scotland and instead made a name for himself with Elgin City, where he topped the goalscoring charts on a regular basis. Jim was another 'cheeky chappie' who had a great personality and a quick wit. If he felt the referee had made a wrong decision in his opinion, rather than lambast him Jim would question it in such a sarcastic manner you just knew he was taking the piss! Jim's love of the game was such that he was still playing in the Aberdeen Sunday Welfare League well into his 40s. It's always a pleasure when I bump into him and have a natter about the good old days.

Peter Corbett was captain and the mainstay of Inverness Caledonian's defence before they combined forces with city rivals Thistle and joined the Scottish Football League. He was the Willie Miller of the Highland League – a fantastic player and reader of the game, an inspirational captain and he just loved to tell referees where they went wrong. He talked incessantly during matches, inspiring his team-mates and offering advice to the officials.

I remember one game at Huntly with Peter in the latter stages of his career when Eddie Copeland skipped past him and he unceremoniously clipped his heel knowing full well he was never going to catch him. I was not required to call Peter over to issue the obligatory yellow card as he walked across to me and said, 'Corbett, Peter, fill in the time and it won't happen again Mr Gunn.' He was always honest enough to know when he was getting 'done'. Peter eventually became a local councillor for the underprivileged area of Merkinch in Inverness where he did a lot of sterling work for the community. The man was a born leader.

Chico McHardy was one of the hardest players I have ever encountered in non-league football. The Elgin City centre-back at that time was the son-in-law of a refereeing colleague of mine, Ali McDonald, who was a very experienced linesman in the Highland League. Any advice that Ali may have offered to Chico must have gone unheeded as he had a mind of his own, didn't suffer fools gladly and his 'attitude' contributed to the many yellow and red cards he picked up during his career.

I remember being in charge of a Highland League Cup replay between Elgin and Forres Mechanics at Borough Briggs one Monday night. The match was finely poised at 1-1 with a few minutes to play when Chico brought down Mechanics midfielder Donnie McCulloch inside the box to concede a penalty. Donnie dusted himself down, converted the spot-kick and Forres went on to win 2-1. Chico was incensed at the decision and claimed I only gave the penalty to avoid extra time so that I would not miss my train back to Aberdeen. Even when I informed him I had taken my car that evening for that very reason, he was having none of it! Typical Chico and he never changed a bit.

8

ASSISTS AND INCIDENTS

ONE OF the nicest guys I had the pleasure of working with in the game was an ex-RAF serviceman by the name of Gordon Logan.

Although he never progressed to senior level (probably due to his age when starting his refereeing career) Gordon was a stalwart as a linesman in the Highland League and referee locally within the Moray & Banff area at amateur and welfare level. Highly respected among his peers, Gordon worked his way up the ranks to become president of the SFA Moray & Banff Referees Association before being appointed a match supervisor by the governing body.

However, one incident involving a game with Gordon still brings tears of laughter to my eyes every time I think about it.

It was a Highland League fixture at Grant Park, Lossiemouth, between the home side and Huntly.

The manager of Huntly on that particular occasion was ex-Manchester United midfielder John Fitzpatrick, originally from Aberdeen, who unfortunately had his playing career cut short due to a serious knee injury. He was not known for his patience or politeness when dealing with referees and was about to explode at half-time in this match.

There was about a minute left in a mediocre, even first half with the score at 0-0 when the Lossie centre-half broke up a Huntly attack and fired a very strong pass out to the right wing aimed at Drew Ross. Now, Drew was a tricky little player but not the quickest and had no chance of catching the ball. Gordon, doing his usual sterling job as linesman, was following the ball back as it bounced awkwardly on the turf. Despite his heroic attempts to get out of the way to let it run out of play, he only succeeded in knocking it into the path of Ross who dispatched an inch-perfect cross for Ronnie Dunbar to head past John Gardiner in the Huntly goal.

Mayhem ensued. Fitzpatrick went mental on the touchline and the Huntly players were quite bemused as to what they had just witnessed. When I blew for half-time the Huntly manager was waiting for me, shouting all sorts of incoherent abuse as to why the goal should not stand. Fortunately, he was dragged away by one of his assistants before things got out of hand.

Previously, I did not have a lot of time for John Fitzpatrick because of the condescending way he treated officials, in my opinion, living off his association with Manchester United. After this incident I had no respect at all for a man who played with arguably the biggest football club in the world yet didn't have a clue about the rules.

Let me explain. It may well be different in this day and age, but in the late 1980s the Laws of the Game dictated that a linesman was treated the same way as a goalpost or corner flag – part of the game and the field of play. On this occasion Gordon tried desperately to get out of the way of the ball, but as he was running so close to the line it hit him before going out of play, therefore I had no option but to play on and the rest is history.

It really saddens me when I meet experienced football managers and players who don't know the basics.

* * *

In all the games I officiated at Tannadice, rarely did their legendary manager Jim McLean (more about Wee Jim later), who was never a great lover of referees, come into our dressing room for one of his infamous rants. Apart from only one occasion in the late 1980s when Hamilton Accies were the visitors which turned out to be hilarious.

United had recently signed Yugoslavian midfielder Miodrag Krivokapic from Red Star Belgrade and 15 minutes before kick-off there was a knock on the dressing room door. It was Wee Jim asking if he could come in for a quiet word with match ref Jim McCluskey, another top whistler. Mr McLean explained that his new signing was not able to speak any English and asked Jim for a bit of leeway if he needed to call him over for any reason, perhaps using his whistle rather than speak to the player as he would not understand him. He was not looking for any special favours. Jim McCluskey said that wouldn't be a problem.

The game was fairly uneventful with United winning thanks to a Jim McInally strike in the second half. After the end-of-match whistle had sounded and all the traditional shaking of hands was taking place, we were approached by Krivokapic who went firstly up to Jim and said quite clearly in perfect English, 'Good game ref, all the best,' while shaking his hand, then approached me and fellow linesman Davie Doig with the words, 'Good game linesman, all the best,' to both of us. As this was going on I caught Jim McLean from the corner of my eye walking from the dugout to the tunnel at the end of the main stand watching the proceedings in front of him. He did not look a happy chap at all.

The three of us had hardly arrived in the dressing room when there was a loud battering at the door and in burst Wee Jim, veins popping out his neck, ranting, 'What did he say to you, I want to bloody well know!' We were finding it very difficult to contain our amusement when Mr McCluskey informed him of the conversation. 'He has been taking the piss out of me for months,' Wee Jim raged. 'These bastards have been teaching him English all this time and never told me. They will pay for this, literally!' Mr McLean was renowned for fining his players sums of money for infringing the club rules, no matter how trivial the perceived offence.

It turned out he was correct. Miodrag's team-mates had been teaching him to speak English but told him he must not tell the boss and any time he spoke to him just to shrug his shoulders in a 'I do not understand' kind of way. Absolutely brilliant.

* * *

Another ground I particularly enjoyed officiating at was Bellslea Park, home of Fraserburgh FC in the Highland League. Commonly known as 'The Broch', it was a very friendly club where you were always invited into the boardroom after the match for a dram and a chat regardless of the result. Their committee was headed up by chairman Jim Adams and secretary Hebbie Scott, an absolute gentleman and a legend for his club and the Highland League in general.

There is always one individual who spoils it for everyone else and after a meaningless, end-of-season 0-0 draw with Elgin City the actions of a guy who had obviously partaken in a few alcoholic beverages before the game could have had very serious consequences indeed for Fraserburgh Football Club.

After a very drab encounter was completed, the players, my linesmen Peter Watson and Jim Bruce, and I headed towards the tunnel. As the match referee I would always allow the players to head in first, followed by the linesmen and then myself. However, on this occasion, Jim was in front of me and Peter behind. I was about to enter the tunnel when I was aware of a minor commotion behind me but kept on walking.

When we arrived in the dressing room Peter asked me if I knew what had happened as we came off the pitch. I said I was aware of something going on behind me but didn't think anything of it. What Peter said to me came as a bit of a shock. He informed me that as we approached the tunnel a young man had jumped out from the stand enclosure and tried to aim a punch at me, but as he slipped and missed, Peter was able to brush him away to allow me to get safely inside.

The question for me now was – was I going to do anything about it? Without going into too much detail, after a discussion with Peter it was decided that as no real harm had been done we would just let the 'incident' go. Jim was very quiet and said nothing, which at the time was a slight concern, as I never knew what was going through that guy's mind, but I got him to agree that no further action would be taken.

In the mid-1970s there had been an incident at Christie Park, Huntly, where someone ran on to the pitch and assaulted referee George McRae, ironically a solicitor from Fraserburgh, and their ground was closed by the SFA for six months.

If the 'incident' had been a lot worse I probably would have had to report it to the SFA, but I certainly did not want to be responsible for the Broch having their ground closed for a period of time due to the actions of one drunken lout who couldn't even aim a decent punch.

After we showered and changed, we made our way to the boardroom for a welcome refreshment, as Hebbie had invited us, as usual, when he handed in the team lines before the start. It quickly became apparent that the committees of both clubs and invited guests were totally unaware of any 'incident' which had taken place at the end of the game, therefore nothing was said, we enjoyed our drinks, said our farewells and made our way home.

By Sunday lunchtime I had decided to forget about the whole thing and move on as I didn't really regard it as a big deal. However, the jungle drums had obviously been beating in Fraserburgh over Saturday night and by Sunday morning had reached the ears of the Broch hierarchy. At about 3pm I received a telephone call at my house from Hebbie Scott asking if I was okay and enquiring about what had actually happened. Hebbie's concern for me was genuine and I also knew he would have been worried about any repercussions that his club may have incurred from the authorities.

I am not going to reveal any details of the conversation we had, but suffice to say, Hebbie was delighted at the outcome when we both put down our phones.

'Incident' over. Next game!

* * *

Another ex-Highland League manager I had admiration and respect for was Dave Watson, an uncompromising centre-half in his playing days with Huntly and Buckie Thistle, where he went on to become boss before moving to Cove Rangers and then Peterhead.

Big Dave was very passionate about his football and always stood up for his teams and players but he was also a very disciplined and fair man, as I was about to find out after a match between Cove Rangers and Ross County at Cove's home ground of Allan Park on the outskirts of Aberdeen.

Ross County were managed at that time by legendary ex-Dundee full-back Bobby Wilson, who I knew very well as he lived in Elgin around the same time as myself, when he managed Keith FC.

If my memory serves me correctly, the game itself was a nothing-at-stake, end-of-season encounter with little on show to excite the sparse crowd on the terracing. The score was 1-1 with a couple of minutes left when I awarded Ross County a free kick in the middle of the pitch for a foul by Cove left-back David Whyte, who immediately got up and right in my face said, 'You're nothing but a fuckin' cheat!' before cowardly running away like a wee schoolboy.

Now, the foul itself was not a particularly bad one, but a foul nonetheless and had Whyte turned his back and muttered any kind of oaths directed to me under his breath without using the word 'cheat' then I probably would have totally ignored it. The fact that he got right in my face and called me 'a fuckin' cheat' with such venom led me to call him back and immediately show him a red card for foul and abusive language.

The match finished 1-1 and as we were coming off the park Bobby Wilson came over to me and said that he thought the dismissal was a bit harsh, but he had not heard what the player had said and walked on.

My fellow officials and I had just returned to our dressing room when there was a loud knock at the door. I opened it and there stood Dave Watson with a face like thunder. 'Can I have a word with you please?' he uttered as he came into the room and shut the door behind him. 'Of course, Mr Watson,' I replied, 'what can I do for you?' I could sense that big Dave was obviously quite angry, but also in control of his emotions. 'Can you please tell me why you sent off my player?' he demanded.

I replied very clearly, 'That is very simple Mr Watson, he called me "a fuckin' cheat".'

Dave was a wee bit taken aback by my response and said he would look into it and get back to me, then left the room.

A few minutes later there was another knock on the dressing room door. It was Dave for the second time and I wrongly assumed he was looking for round two. However, his words have stayed with me until this day, 'Mr Gunn, my player has admitted to me that he called you "a fuckin' cheat" and I have informed him that this is totally unacceptable behaviour within this football club. I have also fined him two weeks' wages and warned all my other players the same would happen to them if there was any repeat of this kind of language to any official in the future.' He then shook my hand, thanked me and wished me all the best for the future. An absolute gentleman.

I only wish I could say the same for his chairman at that time, Alan McRae, but I can't. I will explain my reasons why later in this book.

9

MORE OF THE MAIN MEN

I HAVE already mentioned one or two people who have carried out sterling work on behalf of their clubs over many years, and there are quite a few more to speak about.

One man who stands head and shoulders above anyone else is none other than the late Jock Macdonald, OBE.

Jock, renowned chairman of Inverness Thistle and managing director of Tomatin Distillery, was the doyen of football in the north of Scotland for many years, serving as Highland League president, SFA councillor and many other important positions to help further the game in that area. He was one of the major stakeholders in setting up the merger between his club and Inverness Caledonian to form Inverness Caledonian Thistle to be able to progress to the Scottish Football League in 1994. It was a very challenging time for both clubs as many supporters were against joining forces and to this day there are still some who will not set foot inside the Caledonian Thistle Stadium. During this tough period, Jock worked tirelessly and diligently to push through what he saw was for the greater good of football in Inverness and the surrounding area. He was appointed the inaugural chairman of ICT for his endeavours and the main stand at their stadium is now named after him.

The first time I came across Jock was when he was guest speaker at a meeting of the Moray & Banff Referees Association, where he regaled us with many tales of his involvement within the game at local, national and international levels as he represented the north of the country as an SFA councillor for 21 years, serving on the referee and international committees among others. I remember one story he told was when he was on international duty with Scotland in Poland many years previous, travelling on the team bus from the airport to their hotel. He informed us that he had never witnessed such abject poverty on that route and it was said with so much humility that you knew it had a great effect on Jock.

As a referee, the first time I came into contact with Jock was at Princess Royal Park, home of Deveronvale, who his beloved Jags were due to take on that afternoon. There had been overnight frost and as a precaution Deveronvale had asked local referee Pete Samuel to inspect the pitch on the morning of the game and he, in his wisdom, declared it playable.

When my linesmen and I arrived at the ground about an hour and a half prior to kick-off, we immediately went out to have a look at the pitch. Despite it being a clear, sunny day many areas were rutted and quite hard indeed. This was not looking good at all. Why had Pete Samuel declared this pitch playable? I could only assume that having the backbone of a jellyfish he had bowed down to the fact that the home side were desperate to get the game played, probably for financial reasons more than anything else.

By this time the Inverness Thistle contingent had arrived by coach and the players and officials were having a good look at the playing surface. I could hear the mumblings and grumblings about them not being happy about playing on that. Eventually, I could see Jock making a beeline for me. Now, at no time did he try to influence me in any way, all he did was ask me what my thoughts were. I said to him quite clearly, 'The pitch is rutted and quite hard in large areas and to that end I am declaring it unplayable.' The Jags supremo nodded his head and replied, 'You are absolutely correct Mr Gunn and you will have our complete backing on this. I don't know what that silly bugger Samuel was thinking of.' I could have gladly told him.

On another occasion when we came into close contact, the weather was also a determining factor. It was mid-December in the late 1980s and I travelled up by train to referee a local derby between Inverness Thistle and Clachnacuddin at Kingsmills Park. I found out before travelling that all other Highland League games that day had been postponed because of snow or frost. I remember that 100-plus-mile train journey well as I saw snow, then there was no snow but hard frost, and then more snow. However, on the last lap of my trip between Nairn and Inverness there was no snow at all and everything seemed to be okay. As the train approached the station I just happened to look across to the Black Isle and there was this massive dark cloud lurking. I didn't give it much thought at the time, but it was going to come into play later in the day.

The game kicked off in perfect conditions and, as expected, it was keenly contested with Clach taking an early lead through Mike Paul and Tich Black equalising for the Jags midway through the half. By this time it had started to snow, slow and steady to start with but getting increasingly heavy as half-time approached.

At the interval, as the lines were now becoming invisible, I asked the Thistle ground staff to try and clear the snow as much as they could so that the game could continue. I went into the dressing room for five minutes for my cuppa and then back out again wearing my big trench coat to see how the lads were getting on. Well, as quick as they were clearing the lines in front of them, the snow was belting down and covering them just as bloody quickly!

It was an impossible situation and as I wearily approached the tunnel resembling a snowman, Jock, with the knowledge that the decision to abandon the match was a foregone conclusion, was standing there with a wry smile on his face and said, 'You did your best Mr Gunn but the elements have beaten you. Get yourself showered and changed then come into the boardroom for a dram to heat yourself up!' I think it may have been the only time I was invited in there.

Jock had a reputation for being a hard-nosed businessman and football administrator, which he was, but he was also a very fair and humble man who I had the greatest respect for. He will always be sorely missed by everyone involved in north football.

* * *

During my time in the Highland League I met quite a few players who would go on to bigger and better things. **Colin Hendry** was one such individual whom I first came across playing for junior club Islavale at the tender age of 15. A team-mate of his at that time was a guy called Drew Herbertson, who went on to become the head of the referees' department at the Scottish Football Association.

Even then Colin was a big lump of a laddie who could play equally well at centre-half or up front leading the line. It wasn't long before he moved up a grade to Keith in the Highland League where he spent a couple of seasons before transferring to Dundee in the Scottish Premier League. Incidentally, the Dark Blues signed him as a centre-forward before moving him back to the centre of defence, where he excelled for the rest of his career with Blackburn Rovers, Manchester City, Rangers and, of course, as 'Captain Braveheart' of Scotland, winning 51 caps for his country.

I always got on well with Colin as he was polite and mannerly in his youth and always showed great respect. I remember when he was with Dundee they played neighbours United one Wednesday night at Dens Park in a league fixture which I was attending as a spectator. I parked my car near the ground and was walking down Provost Road on the way to meet some friends when I bumped into Colin and one of his colleagues who he shared digs with. We stood and chatted for a while and Colin, being the nice guy he was, offered me a complimentary ticket for the game. I politely declined, saying I already had one organised. The game was pay at the gate anyway, so there was no problem for me, but if I had taken up the big man's offer I would have ended up in the Dundee end. Not a good idea at all! By the way, United won 4-1 with Colin scoring the Dee's consolation counter.

Another ex-Scottish international I came up against was **John McGinlay,** originally from Fort William, but played for Nairn County over two short spells and Elgin City in the Highland League. He was a prolific goalscorer for both, hitting the net on 63 occasions in just short of 100 appearances. I recall him being a moaning little sod but he was also a bit of a joker which gave him his cheeky personality. John moved down to England where he made his name with Bolton

Wanderers, scoring over 100 goals and gaining 13 caps for his country during his spell there.

Fort William seemed to be a breeding ground for professional footballers as another of its favourite sons, **Duncan Shearer,** also went on from there to have a long and successful career. I remember him when he started out in the Highland League with Clachnacuddin before getting a big move down to England with Chelsea. Despite spending three years there he never quite made it but had successful spells at Huddersfield and Swindon before moving back up north to Aberdeen where he scored 55 goals in a five-year stint. He also made seven appearances for Scotland during his spell with the Dons before ending his playing career at Inverness Caledonian Thistle.

I have known goalkeeper **Nicky Walker** since he was a teenager playing in the Elgin Boys Club set up at the very beginning of my refereeing career. He was also a member of the Walkers of Aberlour family business, world renowned for making the finest shortbread. Nicky started out with Elgin City before being signed aged 18 by former Rangers manager Jock Wallace, then at Leicester City. The same man brought Nicky back up the road to Motherwell where he spent a season. He then enjoyed a long career with other clubs such as Rangers, Hearts, Partick Thistle, Aberdeen, Ross County and Inverness Caledonian Thistle spanning a period of 20 years. He made two appearances for his country during this time. I have met Nicky on quite a few occasions over the years and found him to be an absolute gentleman.

* * *

I like to think I get on with most people I come across in life. However, there will always be exceptions for whatever reason. One man in particular that I have crossed swords with on a few occasions is Mr Cove Rangers, Alan McRae, who later went on to become president of the Scottish Football Association.

Now, don't get me wrong, McRae has given over 50 years' service as a player, committee member and chairman to his club and I have no doubt he worked tirelessly helping them to come up through the ranks from amateur, junior and Highland League levels to their current position within the SPFL. He was also renowned for knowing every rule book ever written on Scottish football inside out. That does not necessarily make him a good guy. I always felt that McRae looked down and sneered at people who could not help him to further his own ends. The fact that he was at one time a councillor for the Conservative Party in Aberdeen did not endear himself to this staunch socialist.

An example of taking the rule book to the limit was at an Aberdeenshire Cup tie being played at an extremely windy Victoria Park in Buckie one Wednesday evening between Buckie Thistle and McRae's Cove Rangers. The match was refereed by an old mate of mine, Ray McNab, who in my opinion was one of the best up-and-coming prospects from the north-east and should have gone all the way to the very top.

Given the wind there was no chance of any decent football being played as it was a venue which was very exposed to the elements. Predictably, the contest ended 0-0 after extra time which meant penalty kicks had to be taken to settle it. However, the gale was so bad that the ball would not sit on either of the penalty spots, despite the efforts of the referee and the players.

Ray then had a wee brainwave. He called in both captains and asked them if they would be happy with a team-mate lying on the pitch with a finger on the ball, only releasing it when the penalty takers were on the point of shooting. Both captains, with the knowledge that a replay would be the only other option, agreed with Ray that this would be the most common-sense approach. Buckie won the shoot-out 5-4, and the players all shook hands and accepted the result.

However, there was always going to be one individual who would not take this lying down – Mr Rule Book himself, Alan McRae. On behalf of his club he protested to the SFA that the rules only permitted the penalty taker and opposing goalkeeper to be in the penalty area during a shoot-out, which although technically correct, seemed to be more than a little childish when his own team captain had readily agreed to a very logical approach by the referee. The appeal was upheld and the game was replayed at a later date. I neither know nor care who won that match because of what happened to Ray at the end of that season.

Ray was not just an excellent referee but one of the nicest guys in the game with his laid-back style and nature. When the Official List of Referees for the next season was announced in June that year Ray was not just demoted but deleted from the list altogether! Absolutely unbelievable as the man, in the opinion of many people in football, was one of the best referees in the north of Scotland. There is no doubt in my mind that Alan McRae's influence had a lot to do with Ray's demise. Ironically, around about this time McRae was vying to get on to some of the SFA's committees. Coincidence? Coincidence my arse!

Below is a saying that was given to me many years ago by a man who is already mentioned in this book and I have used it in all walks of my life, including my trade union days within the newspaper and printing industries. Here it is:

'RULES ARE FOR THE *GUIDANCE OF WISE MEN* AND FOR THE *OBEDIENCE OF FOOLS*'

We all know which category Alan McRae falls into.

One particular match where the man yet again fell down in my estimation was a League Cup final at Kynoch Park, Keith, between Cove and Elgin City, where the then SFA secretary Jim Farry was in attendance. I was the stand-side linesman to Mike Pocock and have to say it was a thoroughly enjoyable match until Elgin scored what proved to be the winning goal for a 2-1 result. The man on target was a guy called John Teasdale, a local character in Elgin, who went on to play in the United States and became a big pal of rock star Rod Stewart when he turned out for the same local team Rod played for in America. The claim from Cove was that Teasdale had been offside when he scored the goal. He couldn't have been more onside if he tried and Mike Pocock agreed when we discussed the incident after the game. Things then blew up as I ran back to the halfway line to take up my position. Ian Chalmers, the assistant manager to Dave Watson at Cove, gave me such a volley of abuse that I had no option but to put up my flag for Mike to come across and send him to the stand for foul and abusive language.

Along with the committee members from both teams we were invited into the boardroom for refreshments after the game. It was then that McRae headed towards me making all sorts of snide remarks about favouring Elgin because he assumed I had come from that area as I started my refereeing career there. He continued to try and goad me into a response, with Pocock getting in between McRae and myself and giving me sound advice about not getting involved. Eventually, two of Cove's other committee members, Alex Walker and Dennis Noughtman, took McRae's arm and ushered him out of harm's way. Alex and Dennis were good, honest guys and Dennis came back a little later to apologise for his chairman's behaviour. I told Dennis not to worry as it didn't bother me what McRae thought, but underneath I was seething as he had come as close to calling me a cheat as he could and that is something I just would not tolerate.

Things eventually came to a head between McRae and I in the famous Grill Bar in Aberdeen's Union Street one Saturday night.

With a former work colleague and good friend of mine, Doug Fisher from Dundee, I had been enjoying a few drinks in the company of referees and some other local football people for a couple of hours in an area of the bar near the door known as 'referees' corner'. I had just started to wear glasses at the time as I needed them for some tasks, although I did wear contact lenses when on refereeing duty but always took them out after my games and put my specs back on.

It was getting close to chucking out time and the bar was starting to empty as some punters were moving on to the city's nightclubs when the bold Mr McRae walked in. It appeared as if he was looking for someone when I must have caught his eye. He then proceeded to lay into me about my eyesight and refereeing abilities in a very personal manner which really upset my mate Doug. The company we shared were a little taken aback, but not in the least surprised by his behaviour.

Although I was absolutely seething with anger, I kept my head and with the knowledge that McRae was certainly not the most popular character in Aberdeen, I calmly said to him, 'Alan, are you looking for a mate in here by any chance?' 'Yes,' he replied, still looking around the bar area. Without showing any emotion at all I ended the conversation by saying to him, 'Well, Alan, you have no mates in this town, now fuck off!' The whole bar fell about laughing at this arrogant chancer being pulled down a peg or two in one of Aberdeen's best-known bars in front of quite a few other football people.

Off he jolly well fucked and never spoke to me again, for which I am eternally grateful!

10

BEGINNING OF THE END

IN THE early 1990s I was made redundant from my job at an oil magazine and subsequently embarked on a new career as a sales representative for a large insurance company with a lot of work being done in the evenings, visiting clients in their own homes after their work.

This made it increasingly difficult for me to juggle the time for training and midweek matches so I was put under a little bit of pressure from my employers to curtail my refereeing activities. I was determined to keep on my football involvement and tried to work as hard as I could at my new job. I saw it out for a couple of years and by this time my then supervisor Bill Crichton was looking to push me for promotion from Grade 3A to Grade 2 as I had progressed quite well. This was never going to be possible with my work situation as moving up to this grade would have meant more midweek appointments at Scottish reserve and youth league fixtures. I spoke at length to Bill about my predicament and suggested to him that it would be better for all if he pushed Ray McNab instead. Ray got promoted at the end of that season and I stayed where I was. I was genuinely pleased for Ray as a friend and colleague as he thoroughly deserved it.

Also, at this time the Highland League began using the services of top referees from all over Scotland, which meant fewer appointments for all the local guys based in the north and north-east, including myself. It may well have been good for the Highland League to use people like Brian McGinlay, Les Mottram, Dougie Hope and the like but it did nothing for the development of up-and-coming local referees.

As I was spending more time back in the junior leagues in the Aberdeen area, I felt I was going backwards. This, coupled with my work commitments and the very sudden death of my father, who had been very supportive throughout my career, led to my resignation from the SFA Senior List. I'd had a great time during my stint, worked with some excellent referees and met a lot of different characters along the way. No axe to grind, just time to go.

I didn't referee at all during the rest of that season and instead joined the local branch of the Dundee United Supporters' Club, the Angus Arabs. Their coach also picked up fans in Montrose and Arbroath travelling to Tannadice and beyond to attend all matches.

United had just built a new stand, named after former chairman George Fox, with the money they got for the transfer of Duncan Ferguson to Rangers and I bought a season ticket that I still have to this day, right on the halfway line – George Fox Lower, Row R, Seat 100 – mine until the day I die.

I also went back to refereeing in the Aberdeen Sunday Welfare League, which was a massive difference to the Highland League and running the line in the Scottish Leagues, but it was quite enjoyable, nonetheless.

11

THE NEW FIRM

ALTHOUGH I did not purchase my season ticket at Tannadice until after I retired from the SFA Senior List in the mid-1990s, I had followed their fortunes for decades; taking in all the cup finals, glamour European ties during the glory years throughout the 1980s and any other match I was able to attend when either not working or refereeing.

By now I tended to see decisions on the field from a referee's point of view, not just a fan's, which I most certainly did as a teenager and in my early 20s.

The 1980s was a fantastic era for Scottish football with the emergence of the 'New Firm' of Dundee United and Aberdeen to challenge the 'Old Firm' of Celtic and Rangers. During this period United won the Scottish Premier League once, were runners-up in the Scottish Cup on no fewer than four occasions, lifted the Scottish League Cup twice and were finalists another twice, reached the semi-final of the European Cup and were defeated in the final of the UEFA Cup in 1987.

Aberdeen's haul was even bigger, winning the league three times (runners-up on another three occasions), being five-time winners of the Scottish Cup, League Cup once and beaten finalists on another three occasions. They also won the European Cup Winners' Cup and UEFA Super Cup in 1983 and reached the semi-finals of the Cup Winners' Cup the following year.

Both clubs at that time had, arguably, the best squads of players in the country coupled with Jim McLean being at the helm at Tannadice and Alex Ferguson managing Aberdeen.

It really was a great period in the history of the Scottish game for everyone involved – players, officials, sponsors and fans – as crowds increased dramatically to witness this new era.

I was refereeing during that time so it felt good to be part of it all, particularly travelling to watch the midweek European ties. I was still living and working in Elgin up until 1985 and regularly made the trip to Tannadice with two fellow Arabs, Doug Fisher and Jimmy Noble. Doug worked alongside me at the *Northern Scot* and in order for us to attend these games we would have to start work at six o'clock in the morning to finish our shift early. Jimmy, who had been a decent full-back for Rothes in the Highland League and player-manager of Fochabers in the North Juniors, worked as a parts manager for a local motor dealer. He would get one of their cars, with a full tank of petrol, pick Doug and I up and we would be on our way south just after two in the afternoon.

We witnessed some amazing performances and victories against sides such as Borussia Monchengladbach, Werder Bremen, Anderlecht, PSV Eindhoven and Standard Liege. The pick of the bunch was the 2-0 defeat of AS Roma in the first leg of the European Cup semi-final in 1984. The atmosphere was electric and I really believed United were good enough to go on and lift the trophy that season.

What happened in the second leg has been well documented in other publications and it is too painful for me to go over it in detail again. However, the main points were that the final was to be played at Roma's home ground, the Olympic Stadium, and they would stoop to just about anything to achieve their goal.

Referee Bob Valentine with Dundee and Dundee United captains Bobby Glennie and Paul Hegarty prior to the Scottish League Cup Final in 1980

Aberdeen celebrate winning the European Cup Winners' Cup in 1983

Duncan Shearer, former Aberdeen striker who started his career in the Highland League

Jim McLean and Alex Ferguson

Dundee United manager Jim McLean with his players after winning the Scottish Premier League in 1983

Eddie Thompson shortly after taking ownership of Dundee United

Scene of my European appointment at Dynamo Berlin

Robbie Harrold, former refereeing colleague and supervisor

The famous Hedge at Brechin City

Dundee United v Gothenburg, UEFA Cup Final 1987

Andrew Waddell awarding THAT penalty to Hearts against Dundee United in 1989 (DC Thomson)

Scottish Junior FA president and old friend Jim Grant (bottom right) officiating at the Scottish Junior Cup draw in the 1990s (DC Thomson)

Victorious Dundee United after defeating Rangers in the Scottish Cup Final 1994

Eddie Thompson, shown on the big screen at Hampden Park during the 2008 Scottish League Cup Final against Rangers

FIFA referee Brian McGinlay in action at Tannadice (**DC Thomson**)

Dundee United after beating Ross County in the 2010 Scottish Cup Final

Long-serving
Fraserburgh manager
and Highland League
legend Charlie Duncan
(DC Thomson)

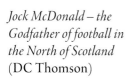

Jock McDonald – the
Godfather of football in
the North of Scotland
(DC Thomson)

George Stephen celebrating scoring for Peterhead (DC Thomson)

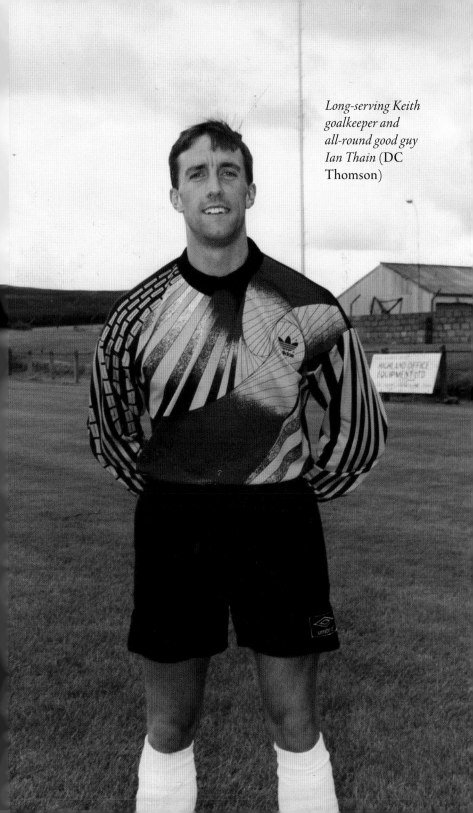

Long-serving Keith goalkeeper and all-round good guy Ian Thain (DC Thomson)

My guide and mentor Sandy Roy administering a yellow card to Dundee United skipper Maurice Malpas (DC Thomson)

2016 League Cup Final v Celtic

They unsuccessfully attempted to bribe French match referee Michel Vautrot, incidentally a good friend of Bob Valentine, who went on to take charge of the 1986 European Cup Final between Barcelona and Steaua Bucharest.

The Italians won 3-0 but the intimidation suffered by United's players and officials before, during and after the game, was nothing short of a disgrace. My old mate John Gardiner, who was on the bench for United that night, told me he had never been so scared in his life and John is a big hardy lad.

Ironically, the Tangerines' midfield dynamo Billy Kirkwood had an excellent chance to score after 17 minutes to kill the tie stone dead as Roma would have needed to find the net on five occasions to go through.

Thankfully, they lost the final on penalties to Liverpool and I have hated those cheating bastards ever since.

It was a bonus if United were away from home when Aberdeen played their home European ties at Pittodrie as I would travel through to watch these games with my refereeing colleagues Sandy Roy and Gordon Logan. I also witnessed some brilliant performances from the Dons including victories against teams such as Ipswich Town, Lech Poznan, SV Hamburg and a major highlight in the European Cup Winners' Cup quarter-final against Bayern Munich. Outside of watching Dundee United, this was the best atmosphere I have ever witnessed at Pittodrie. Aberdeen went 1-0 down early on and then 2-1 behind with minutes to go. I remember turning round to Sandy and saying, 'I think their chance is gone now, Big Man,' or words to that effect. I had hardly finished my statement when, all of a sudden, the ground burst into a crescendo of noise. Now, this was quite unusual for Aberdeen as their fans were not renowned for their vocal support. The joke was you were more likely to hear the rustle of sweetie papers than the crowd urging their team on. Not on this occasion, however, as Aberdeen went on to win the tie 3-2 with goals from Alex McLeish and John Hewitt. One of the best games I have seen at Pittodrie.

Despite the fact that United did not win a European trophy their overall record during the 1980s was the best of any of the Scottish clubs including two consecutive UEFA Cup quarter-finals, one European Cup semi-final and the UEFA Cup Final. A remarkable achievement.

12

SCOTTISH CUP
SUCCESS AT LAST

IN 1991 United again reached the final of the Scottish Cup, this time against Motherwell, who were managed by Jim McLean's brother Tommy, and I took my son and daughter down to Hampden to witness the most epic showpiece of the season encounter which has ever been played at the old ground. It was end-to-end football with numerous chances being created and lots of talking points debated throughout the entire match. Motherwell ended up 4-3 winners after extra time.

Our seats were in the main stand at the national stadium and as referee David Syme blew the final whistle, I stood up hand-in-hand with my kids ready to make a quick exit. My son Kevin, who was eight years old at the time, had sensed my obvious disappointment and despair at yet another defeat in a Scottish Cup final, tugged on my arm and said to me, 'But Dad, at least it was a great game!' That small statement put everything into perspective for me. The wee man had thoroughly enjoyed the match, and in his world, that was all that mattered. He was correct, of course, but this died-in-the-wool Arab was going to take some convincing.

In 1994 United reached their seventh Scottish Cup Final in 20 years. They were to play Rangers who were chasing back-to-back trebles. This looked like the toughest ask since their first final in 1974 against Celtic as they had finished the league in mid-table, 16 points and 34 goals of a difference behind their opponents.

Despite this, United had hammered Rangers at their own Ibrox ground the previous December, racing to a three-goal lead after just 21 minutes which they kept until the end. A few weeks before the final United were again 1-0 up at Ibrox when they were denied a stonewall penalty with around ten minutes to go. Gordon Durie scored two late goals for the home side and United were defeated 2-1.

Ivan Golac, a former Southampton and Yugoslavia full-back, had been appointed United's new manager at the start of that season as Jim McLean had retired from his coaching duties but remained chairman and major shareholder of the club. Ivan was a completely different character from Wee Jim – confident and laid back, instilling belief in his players. His idea of a pre-match warm-up was to take the team for a walk in the park and smell the flowers. Some fans were certain he was on the 'wacky baccy'!

The game itself was not a classic with Craig Brewster scoring the vital goal on 46 minutes after a mix-up in the Rangers defence. For most of the remainder of the second half it was like the Alamo with United defending heroically at times as Rangers chased that elusive equaliser. After what seemed an eternity, referee Dougie Hope blew the final whistle and they had done it, United had won the Scottish Cup for the first time in their history at the seventh time of asking. I was absolutely ecstatic, my team having finally completed the feat of winning all three domestic trophies.

The celebrations went on for about a week and one of my abiding memories after the game was travelling through Rutherglen in our supporters' coach en route to the motorway north, with hundreds of Celtic fans out on the streets or hanging out of their tenement windows waving their scarves to cheer us on. That is

Glasgow for you and little did I know I would be living there many years later.

United entered a bit of a lean spell after that, were relegated at the end of the next season and spent one season in the First Division before coming straight back up via a 3-2 aggregate success against Partick Thistle in the play-offs.

It was to be 2005 before they reached another Scottish Cup Final and yet another defeat at the hands of Celtic. An early Alan Thomson strike was enough to give the Glasgow giants the trophy for the fourth time against United. A Celtic-daft mate of mine, Alex McMillan, has always said to me, 'You will never beat Celtic in the sunshine at Hampden.' Up to the present time he has been proved absolutely correct.

Ross County, who had only been promoted from the Highland League to Scottish League Division Three in 1994, rocked football in April 2010 by beating Celtic 2-0 in their semi-final to reach the Scottish Cup Final for the first time in their history. Their opponents were to be none other than Dundee United.

It was fantastic being part of a great family atmosphere at Hampden that day with County taking down just short of 20,000 fans from the north of Scotland. This was an amazing feat as their base in Dingwall, 15 miles north of Inverness, only had a population of under 6,000 inhabitants. Their fan base did stretch across the Black Isle and beyond and it was reckoned quite a few Invernessians made the journey down to cheer on their neighbours as well.

Just as remarkable was the size of the United support, with 28,000 making the trip from the City of Discovery, which defies logic as the average support at Tannadice that season was just under 9,000 – and that includes away fans.

United ran out comfortable 3-0 winners with second-half goals from David Goodwillie and Craig Conway (2) and the club lifted the trophy for the second time.

At the time of writing the last time Dundee United reached the final at Hampden was in 2014 where their opponents were Tayside rivals St Johnstone. The club finished just two places above Saints in the league that season and, as always, it was going to be a tough, close encounter.

That was exactly how it turned out with United missing several chances throughout the 90 minutes and the Perth side taking theirs to run out 2-0 winners.

If there was one team I would not begrudge any success to it would be the Perth Saints. This was the first domestic trophy they had lifted in their 130-year history, so it was a momentous occasion for all connected with the club and they thoroughly deserved their celebrations.

13

COMING OUT
OF RETIREMENT

SATURDAY, 13 September 1997 is a day that will be forever etched in my memory. I had been retired from the Official List of SFA Referees for a few years and was in my usual seat at Tannadice to watch Dundee United take on Kilmarnock in a Scottish Premier League match.

Kilmarnock had taken an early lead and it stayed that way until half-time. As I was having a chat with some of the lads in the concourse of the George Fox Stand during the interval, there was a tannoy announcement to ask if there were any qualified referees available to run the line as Ian Taylor, the match referee from Edinburgh, had picked up an injury during the first half which was serious enough for him to stay inside the dressing room.

Usually in attendance there would be one or two senior listed members of the Angus & Perth Referees' Association who didn't have a game that day and they would offer their services. However, almost ten minutes later the same announcement was repeated. One of my best mates and a United legend as a fan, Shuggy Falconer, whose seat was next to mine, came up the stairs and shouted to me to get my backside across to the referees' room to help out. On my way there I had to run past half of the George Fox Stand and the East Stand, as it was known then, and there were quite a few people with seats there who knew me quite well. They roared me on for a bit of banter.

On my arrival at the dressing room, accompanied by a steward who was making sure I was for real, I was met by George Smith, the SFA referee supervisor for the match, and the three officials. I knew George reasonably well as I had run the line for him on a few occasions. In fact, he was the referee in my first Scottish League match as a linesman, Forfar Athletic's 4-0 thrashing of St Johnstone in September 1984. George recognised me immediately and asked how long I had been retired. I told him and he said, 'Right, get stripped and let's get this second half under way as soon as possible.' I borrowed Ian Taylor's kit and went out and did the job I was supposed to do without any major problems at all, although I did feel my calf muscles beginning to tighten towards the end as I hadn't really trained for a couple of years. United lost 2-1 to a controversial penalty given to Kilmarnock by the replacement referee John Underhill in the other half of the field of play from me. I was standing at the halfway line and my strong opinion was Killie's French forward Jerome Varielle had played his trailing leg on to United keeper Sieb Dykstra's outstretched arms rather than the other way around. In the dressing room John made the mistake of asking my opinion on the penalty decision. I don't think he was too happy when I told him, 'If that was a penalty I am the Queen of Sheba.' George Smith paid me a big compliment when he said to me, 'John, I would never have thought you'd ever been away from it.'

My supporters' club coach from Aberdeen had to wait for me while I got showered and changed. I got on to rapturous applause and as United had played so poorly the guys and girls even voted me man of the match, an accolade that no other non-United player has ever won.

This story does not end here, however.

During the following week I received a very nice letter from the then secretary of the Scottish Football League, Peter Donald, thanking me for offering my services to help out the match officials. He also stated that there would be a cheque forwarded to me in due course for a half-match fee which amounted to around £35 at the time.

However, as a few weeks had passed and I still hadn't received a cheque, I wrote a letter to Peter telling him about the situation and my concern that it may have either gone missing in the post or not been sent out at all. I asked him to alert his appropriate administrative department to investigate. I also pointed out that at no time did I expect to receive any financial reward for helping out but it was generous of them to offer.

By this time Dundee United had qualified for the Scottish League Cup Final against Celtic at Ibrox Stadium, home of Rangers, at the end of November. It was played there as the national stadium Hampden Park was under redevelopment. I asked if it would be possible, in lieu of any payment, to supply me with three tickets for the match so I could take my son and daughter. That would be far more appreciated. Within three days the tickets arrived in the post with an accompanying letter from Peter stating, 'I anticipated that you would be wanting your tickets to be in the Dundee United end!'

As it turned out the tickets were worth more than the half-match fee and Peter bloody well knew that!

14

FOLLOWING UNITED

WHEN I joined the Dundee United Angus Arabs Supporters' Club we had fewer than 100 members, our coach starting its journey from Aberdeen, down the east coast picking up at Montrose, Arbroath and sometimes Carnoustie. We had gained a good reputation as being a friendly, hospitable bunch and we were an official organisation being affiliated to the Federation of Dundee United Supporters' Clubs, which was recognised by the football club itself.

It wasn't long before we began to get applications for membership from fans residing in the Angus towns of Brechin and Forfar. This became a logistical nightmare for travelling as the coach would have to zig-zag its way down the country from the Granite City to Dundee and beyond, making it a very long day, particularly for away fixtures. Also, as numbers were increasing rapidly, we would sometimes have to put on two coaches to accommodate everyone.

It was decided at our annual general meeting in the summer of 1995 that the Angus Arabs would disband, because it had logistically become too big to run effectively, and two new clubs would be formed. The newly named East Angus Arabs would cater for members who travelled from the route starting at Montrose, down the coast through Arbroath and Carnoustie. Our new club was to be known as the A90 Arab Society (A90 Arabs), starting our journey from Aberdeen, down the A90 trunk road south through Laurencekirk, Brechin and Forfar. I was elected to be the first club chairman which meant I also attended meetings at federation level.

It was a bit of a gamble creating two new supporters' clubs when United had just been relegated from the top league to what was known then as Scottish League Division One, travelling to unfamiliar towns such as Airdrie, Dumbarton and Clydebank. However, as most of our members were season ticket holders, our coach was full most weeks, and we were also attracting new applications from fans who lived in Dundee. Again, this was due to the reputation we had earned and the popularity of our well-known bus convener, the aforementioned Shuggy Falconer. Over the years the Dundee-based supporters referred to our club as 'Shug's Bus'.

Shuggy was, and still is, the epitome of any football fan. He travelled everywhere with United to all domestic and European home and away games AND pre-season friendlies in the UK and abroad. If the team were to organise a friendly on the moon, he would be the first man to phone Tannadice to ask when the shuttle would be leaving! Another man who fell into this category was a dyed-in-the-wool Arab from Dundee, Shug's long-suffering travelling partner to European away ties, Davie Short, an absolute gem of a man.

Our cup-winning manager Ivan Golac had been sacked in March just before relegation, being replaced by former player Billy Kirkwood. Billy did get United promoted back to the Premier League but only lasted a few games into the next season before Jim McLean's brother Tommy took charge.

We had some great trips that season to uncharted territory and eventually came back up to the top league at the first attempt through the play-offs.

Over the years there have been quite a few characters who travelled with the A90 Arabs. One particular gentleman was a retired Merchant Navy captain by the name of Eric Taylor who had many stories to tell of his exploits on the ocean waves. Being a man of the sea, Eric was quite partial to a rum or three (George Morton's OVD to be precise) so got quite tiddly on occasions which led to some amusing situations.

United were playing Raith Rovers at their Starks Park ground in Kirkcaldy in our first season back in the Premier League in 1996. Most of us enjoyed a few beers in a nearby pub with Eric having his fair old quota of OVD. He would also take a flask of 'coffee' with him on the coach which I didn't discover until some time later was probably about 70 per cent proof!

Anyway, with Eric being a wee bit unsteady on his feet, it was decided Shug and I would get a taxi to take the three of us up to the ground. On arrival, Eric nearly fell out of the cab in full view of a policeman standing at the turnstile. When the cop saw he was being accompanied by Shug and myself, he said to us, 'I am going to turn round for a couple of seconds and by the time I turn back I want him in the ground out of my sight.' We carried out his instruction to the letter, but when we got inside, the pie stall was right in front of us. Eric, thinking he was in another bar, walked up to the counter and asked the young assistant for three OVDs! The dismayed look on the girl's face was priceless. Shug and I quickly grabbed Eric and shunted him up the stairs to our seats in the stand behind the goal, where he slept for most of the match. The officer outside the ground could have taken action against old Eric, but probably thought he was in safe hands and would more than likely be very difficult to process back at the station.

On another occasion he caused a stir at Tannadice by accusing a fellow fan of sitting in his seat after he returned from the toilet at half-time. Shug heard the commotion and rushed to the scene before Eric got into serious trouble. It turned out he had gone down the wrong aisle and Shug quickly led him away back to his own seat, offering profuse apologies to the guy and the two stewards who appeared.

On our way home from our travels down to the west of Scotland, our coach would stop in Dunblane for a couple of pints and then collect some food from the nearby chip shop or Chinese takeaway. After a game at Ibrox where we got a draw it was my turn to go to the Chinese to order our meals for the journey home. I picked them up just before departure and had a chicken curry for Eric. On the coach he started to eat before nodding off to sleep with the container in his lap. Now, when Eric fell asleep, his bottom set of false teeth had a habit of slipping out and nestling on his chest. As Shug had witnessed this happen again, he went across to Eric's seat and put his false teeth right in the middle of his curry. When Eric woke up and returned to consume his meal, he suddenly shouted at the top of his voice, 'Gunner, what the hell have you bought me here. This chicken's like a bloody brick!' The whole bus erupted in fits of laughter before the old seaman realised what was going on.

By this time I had attended quite a few meetings of the Federation of Dundee United Supporters' Clubs and had given my fair share of input on matters such as ticket pricing, access for disabled fans, amount of tickets for United fans at all-ticket matches against the big clubs, policing (particularly at away matches) and general topics involving the football club.

Now and again there would be a representative from the club present depending on the topic being discussed. With Jim McLean being chairman and majority shareholder, he was a man who played his cards very close to his chest, so there was very little information coming out which was helpful to the fan base. Wee Jim was very protective of the club he regarded as HIS and not OURS.

At the federation AGM in 1996 I was asked by a good friend of mine from the Tangerine Club in Dundee, Gordon Sturrock, if he could nominate me for the executive committee. I said to Gordon that if he and others thought I could do a job then I would go for it. As it happened, I got voted on as vice-chairman to Jimmy Jardine, another die-hard from the Tangerine Club whom I also knew very well. The secretary, who had been in the post for a few years, was a man who lived in Edinburgh called Jim Gardiner. Jim was a decent enough guy but having retired from a senior position within Scottish Gas, could come across as being a bit superior and pompous in his approach. As he had more time on his hands than the rest of the committee, he tried to form a close, personal relationship with the club, Wee Jim in particular. Although Gardiner would have us believe he had the chairman's ear, Wee Jim kept him at bay, the same as everyone else from outside the football club who would attempt to get their feet under the table.

There was one occasion at a meeting, however, when I totally agreed with Jim McLean. He was asked a question by one of the federation committee about why was it when the Old Firm, Aberdeen and sometimes Hibs and Hearts fans came to Tannadice they would be allocated the traditional United 'Shed End' as well as the main and fair play stands, which gave them around 50 per cent of the total capacity.

Jim pondered for a moment and his answer was, 'If you can guarantee that you can fill that end with United fans you can have it. If you can't, I know and you know, they will.' It was pure economics. It was his responsibility to fill the ground to generate as much income for the club as possible. The matter was never debated.

One of the highlights of the year for Dundee United fans was the Dave Narey Quiz, named after probably the best player ever to have graced Tannadice Park. This event took place in the Tangerine Club towards the end of every season and the A90 Arabs always had a strong four-man team, usually consisting of Keith Wilson, Derek Watson, Shuggy and myself. Over the years we were always in the top three or four teams, then in 2001 we actually won the trophy.

That in itself was a great feat, but more importantly, the recently formed subscription-only ITV Digital had contacted the federation regarding an upcoming quiz show for football supporters throughout the UK called *Do I Not Know That?* and asked if Dundee United fans would like to participate. As we had won the quiz it was decided that the A90 Arabs would represent the Tannadice faithful.

The filming was to take place at Granada Studios in Manchester on Sundays from November through to the end of April. Each team was allowed five members per show, with only three competing at any one time, and substitutions could be made. Simon O'Brien, of Channel Four's *Brookside* fame and a staunch Everton fan, was the compere. Simon was a lovely guy, friendly and quick witted, a proper football man.

The arrangement with the show's producers was that wherever United were playing on the Saturday, after the match the five participants would be picked up by minibus at a pre-arranged point near the ground and driven down to Manchester. We were put up in a hotel in the city centre and given £75 between us for 'sustenance' (which became the kitty for our rounds of drinks). On the Sunday morning we made our way to the studios, filmed one, or sometimes two, episodes and were then driven back up to Scotland. ITV Digital were very accommodating by trying to ensure the furthest team to travel were the first on for filming.

The format was that there were eight groups of five teams, with the top two progressing to the next round which was a straight knockout right through to the final. The teams in our group were Dundee, Hearts, Scunthorpe and Everton.

The lads had some great trips down to Manchester over the next five months, meeting up with fellow fans from many different football clubs, sharing a few beers and stories about their various travels with their teams.

Before one particular visit to the Granada Studios, United were playing a derby match against Dundee at Dens Park where the Tangerines won courtesy of a last-minute own goal from Lee Wilkie. We were allowed to change our team from show to show and on this occasion, Simon Pringle travelled with Derek, Shug and myself. In anticipation of a victory and a good celebration on the way down the road, everyone except Derek had a bottle of OVD in their possession. We arrived in Manchester around 9.30pm, went out to a couple of pubs and met some Hearts fans, who we were competing against the next day. A great night was had by all and we were pretty hungover the next morning as we trooped along to the studios. There was a technical hitch which was to take around half an hour or so to sort out. Simon O'Brien made a point of coming over to have a chat with the teams and when he approached us, he was rather taken aback by the smell on our breath. 'What the hell is that?' he asked, reeling back from the strong alcoholic aroma. 'George Morton's finest OVD rum,' he was informed by Shug. Simon then warned everyone in the studio not to strike up a match for fear of blowing up the building! We gifted him a bottle on our last trip down. I wonder if he enjoyed it?

The team reached the quarter-final where we lost out to eventual winners Wimbledon who were a bunch of anoraks. Instead of going out socialising with the other teams on a Saturday night, they would stay in the hotel and pore through football quiz book questions and various statistics. Fair play to them, it worked in their favour, but even Simon thought it was a bit over-the-top, as the whole contest was meant to be a bit of fun with a coming together of football fans from all over the country.

On that last visit, United were playing Hibs on the Sunday afternoon with a 3pm kick-off and we were to be the first team on at 8am. I asked the organisers if it would be okay on this occasion to hire a car to come down so that we could take in an English game somewhere in Lancashire. This was given the go-ahead and we decided to visit a very important relegation clash between Bolton Wanderers and Ipswich Town, the reason being one of our team members, Davie Bowman, supported Ipswich as his Sassenach team.

The situation prior to the game was if Bolton won, they would stay up and Ipswich get relegated. If Ipswich won or it was a draw, they could both still go down. Shug and I, along with our fellow team-mates on this trip, Mark Dorward and Gordon Anderson, got tickets for the Bolton end, while Davie decided to make his own arrangements and took a seat in the away section of the stadium.

The home side absolutely annihilated Ipswich in the first 45 minutes and were 4-0 up at the break. As the half-time whistle blew, we could see Davie, with a face like thunder, marching down the stand behind the goal, with the knowledge that he would not be taking in the second half. When we met Mr Bowman outside the ground after the match finished 4-0, he produced two bottles of red wine from his inside jacket pockets. No questions were asked where he managed to 'acquire' them, we just enjoyed the free drink!

Incidentally, after our encounter with the Dundee fans in the quiz, we all travelled back up the road together, sharing a few beers on the way. They were a good bunch of lads as it happened.

Having to pay for minibus or car hires, hotel rooms, food and drink for around 200 football fans over a five-month period, it was little wonder ITV Digital went into liquidation in October that year.

15

JIM McLEAN

BEFORE I start this chapter, which may not go down too well with some Dundee United fans, I would like to thank Wee Jim for his contribution to the club – Scottish Premier League winners in 1983, League Cup winners in 1979 and 1980 and a run of European results during that period which was surpassed by no other Scottish club then.

However, there could have been so much more. Many fans and football writers alike have acknowledged Jim as being United's most successful manager. I disagree. McLean was a fantastic coach, probably the best in the country, but his managerial skills were questionable at best. In my opinion he was not a nice man at all, a bully who treated his players like dirt at times. His lack of belief in his own ability spread through to his squad, particularly on the big occasions. One very prominent player during that time told me a few years ago that, on cup final days travelling on the team coach from the hotel to Hampden, Wee Jim would go round the players telling them how difficult it was going to be rather than giving out positive vibes about giving their opponents a bloody good hiding.

Alex Ferguson at Aberdeen was the total opposite; a very good coach but excellent at man-management, realising he had to treat different players in different ways to be able to get the best out of them on the field. He had total belief in his own and his players' abilities to win.

There was no difference between the playing squads at Tannadice and Pittodrie during the 1980s, yet the Dons won more trophies than United. There had to be a reason.

Jim McLean took Dundee United to six Scottish Cup finals during his tenure at Tannadice, losing the lot. Between 1981 and 1991, when they had arguably better teams than our cup final opponents, they lost all five. Two of them were against St Mirren and Motherwell. Now, with no disrespect to those two, they should not have beaten a side with the quality of personnel in United's ranks. The club finished 26 points and a 66-goal difference ahead of St Mirren in the league in 1987 but they still managed to lose 1-0 after extra time in the final. Motherwell were the opponents in 1991 and United completed the league season eight points and 11 goals ahead of our rivals, losing out 4-3, again after extra time. There had to be a reason.

Even when they lost out to Rangers in 1981 and Celtic in 1985 and 1988, United more than matched their squads, losing out to the Ibrox side 4-1 in the replay after a 0-0 draw and suffering two narrow 2-1 defeats to Celtic after being ahead in both games. There had to be a reason.

We Jim's side also narrowly lost two League Cup finals to Rangers who were definitely not the force they once used to be. The scores were 2-1 in 1981 after being ahead and 1-0 in 1984 to an Iain Ferguson goal. There had to be a reason.

I think it is not too much of a coincidence that when United did eventually win the Scottish Cup with Ivan Golac in charge, they finished 18 points and 34 goals behind Rangers in the league that season but triumphed at Hampden. There had to be a reason.

Many will think I am being too hard on Wee Jim, but these are the facts. I firmly believe that had Alex

Ferguson been in charge at Tannadice and McLean at Pittodrie, United would have trebled their trophy haul during that period because of Fergie's winning mentality and man-management skills.

During McLean's term as manager he acquired quite a few shares in the club, either by purchase or gifts from former chairmen or others. He was appointed a director in 1984 and four years later became chairman, managing director and majority shareholder, as well as continuing to manage the team. I regarded this as being very unhealthy, giving one man so much power within one organisation.

After retiring as manager in 1993, Jim appointed Golac as his successor at the start of the next season. United finished sixth in the league and, of course, won the Scottish Cup. During the next eight years with McLean at the helm, the club would be relegated, finish in the bottom half of the Premier League every season except one and appoint another four managers in Billy Kirkwood, Tommy McLean, Paul Sturrock and Alex Smith.

Wee Jim resigned as chairman and a director in 2000 after assaulting BBC radio reporter John Barnes during an interview after a home match against Hearts. Some felt he had been goaded into this act by Barnes's line of questioning. Whatever, there was no reason for the chairman of a football club to resort to bar-room violence, but this was typical of McLean who often lashed out, although mainly verbally, at people who disagreed with – or did not carry out – his explicit instructions.

Although he was no longer chairman, Jim continued as majority shareholder for a further two years, still pulling all the strings, before selling out to local die-hard fan and millionaire businessman Eddie Thompson.

16

THE EDDIE THOMPSON YEARS

DESPITE FINISHING third in the league the previous season, United were involved in yet another relegation battle in 1997/98 and fans were becoming more and more disgruntled at the lack of progress and inconsistency on the field.

On the penultimate day of the season they played Hibs at Easter Road in a do-or-die situation. If United won, they stayed up and almost certainly relegated Hibs. Thanks to two Kjell Olofsson goals they scraped a 2-1 victory to retain their Premier League status. This was United's first win in the league since the beginning of February, a plethora of draws in between times having helped them stay up. At half-time during that match I was approached by fellow Arabs Mike

Watson and Neil Glen who sat behind Shuggy and I at Tannadice. I got to know them very well over the years attending matches home and away. Mike was a Labour MP and Neil was a Labour activist in Dundee.

They informed me that because of the current situation within the club there was to be a rally taking place in a few weeks staged by a new dissident fans' group desperately seeking change within the corridors of power at Tannadice. They also knew I concurred with their views and that, as vice-chairman of the Federation of Dundee United Supporters' Clubs, it would be a good idea for me to attend.

The rally took place in July that year in the grounds of the University of Dundee, and was attended by more than 500 United supporters, not all of whom agreed with the views of the newly formed United for Change (UFC). This was the beginning of a new era for Dundee United Football Club.

It was felt by the group, and many other fans, that things had become extremely stale under the stewardship of Jim McLean. Although he had a board of directors, including long-serving former centre-half and an absolute gentleman, Doug Smith, it was obvious that Jim controlled everything which went on inside the club.

The catchphrase United for Change developed and used to get their message across was, 'New faces, new money, new ideas'. The purpose behind the rally was to give the group publicity and gauge support from fellow Arabs to be able to move forward. A week later UFC held a press conference at Discovery Point with a host of local and national newspapers, along with the BBC and STV television cameras, present to witness the plans we had to turn our hopes into reality.

As well as Mike, Neil and myself, members of the steering group included Derek Robertson (former senior manager with one of the major banks), George Gall (owner of a communications business), Kevin Geoghegan (owner of a print business), Rab Lyon (lecturer at Dundee University), Billy Kay (journalist and broadcaster) and Martin Manzi, all die-hard Dundee United fans.

After the press conference the group adjourned to a conference room in the nearby Hilton Hotel for a meeting. This is when I met Eddie Thompson for the first time and was introduced to what exactly United for Change was attempting to achieve.

Eddie, originally from Glasgow and a qualified accountant, moved to Dundee as a young man and quickly settled into the City of Discovery. He loved his football, watching Motherwell on a regular basis before his move north, and as he had now made Dundee his home chose to go to Tannadice to support United. His association with the club was to become a lot closer throughout the years as he was responsible – through his senior position within parent company Watson & Philip – for VG convenience stores to become shirt sponsors of Dundee United on the run up to the Scottish Cup Final in 1985.

In 1991 he left Watson & Philip to form his own chain of stores named Morning Noon & Night, eventually becoming a self-made millionaire. He was very passionate about Dundee United and his company continued to invest money in the club by way of advertising, hospitality, etc, but like many other fans in the mid-1990s, had become very disillusioned with the direction they had been heading under the chairmanship of Jim McLean.

It was Eddie's desire to buy out Wee Jim's shares and take over the running of the club. He had all the credentials – die-hard fan, close contacts within the club, successful businessman and the ready cash to do so. That meeting in the Hilton was the first of many over the next four years to begin a new chapter in the history of Dundee United. However, the only obstacle in the steering group's way was the man himself, Jim McLean, who most definitely was not going to give up HIS beloved club. It proved to be a long, hard road.

When the pictures of the press conference at Discovery Point were transmitted on the TV that evening, it then became obvious to my colleagues within the federation that I had become entrenched as a member of United for Change.

Jimmy Jardine and Jim Gardiner were staunch McLean fans and were not too happy to see their vice-chairman taking what they saw as an anti-McLean stance in public without consulting them. Gardiner was particularly incensed and called for a meeting of the federation executive to discuss the matter.

That meeting took place in Frews Bar, at the top of Hilltown in Dundee, where Jim Gardiner tore a strip off me for not informing the committee of my intentions and demanding my immediate resignation. I calmly informed him that, despite my position within the federation, I was an individual fan and therefore entitled to my own views. Also, at no time did I indicate publicly I was the federation representative within the pressure group, despite the fact that I was mentioned as being their representative in press and TV reports.

I flatly refused to resign as I had been elected by the member clubs and, if he really wanted to get rid of me, he would have to call a full emergency general meeting to let the membership decide. Despite McLean having a fair bit of loyal support among the fanbase, there was generally a mood for change because of the way things had been going on the field. If Jim Gardiner had called for an EGM to have me removed it would have been very risky indeed. If he lost, his position would have become untenable, and he knew it. He thought better of it.

I have to say, during this time, although Jimmy Jardine and I had opposite views and debated at length during the next couple of years, we never fell out. We had differences of opinion, but both wanted the best for our beloved football club and respected one another for that. Jimmy still sits a couple of rows behind me at Tannadice and we remain friends to this day, usually meeting for a blether at half-time during home matches.

This did not stop Gardiner treating me like a leper, saying I could not be trusted to pass information on to United for Change. He was absolutely correct, of course, as that was exactly what the steering group required. The federation was the only fan group recognised by the club and to have a man 'on the inside' was the perfect scenario to gauge the support United for Change had within it.

As time went on momentum was building among the supporters for changes to take place and the steering group was now making some progress.

United had now employed the services of a PR company called Beattie Media to help them handle this increasingly difficult situation.

There were now regular meetings taking place between the federation, the Dundee United Businessmen's Club (they were present due to their affiliation to McLean) and representatives from the club. Quite a few members from United for Change – Derek Robertson, Neil Glen and Martin Manzi among them – had joined federation member clubs and attended these meetings. Beattie Media were represented at these gatherings by an obnoxious character called Niall Scott, who decided who the 'enemy' were and tried to stare us out in a pathetic attempt at intimidation.

Jim McLean would often attend these meetings, but as he always did, would regale those present with tales of all our yesterdays about matches and players, knowing that some of his audience would be in awe of him and get them onside. He would do anything but discuss the real issues within HIS club, never accepting that it really was time to go.

The federation at no time endorsed the views of United for Change but at every opportunity Jim Gardiner would publicly back Wee Jim and the status quo. I warned him that he was not speaking on behalf of all the members as, by this time, support for the steering group had swelled.

What was required was a meeting to take place for a vote from all member clubs to decide once and for all whether the federation was going to back United for Change or not. The committee agreed that this was the best way forward and a date was set for Sunday, 4 October 1998 in Frews Bar before a televised match against Aberdeen at Tannadice.

There were 21 member clubs of the federation at that time and I had got to know quite a few guys in most of them, particularly at away games where it was the same old faces who would turn up every second week. It was also beneficial having Shuggy Falconer as a right-hand man as he knew two or three times the amount of people I did, and as I have said before, was a very popular and influential guy. He was also a staunch supporter of the steering group.

In the weeks leading up to the meeting there had been a fair bit of canvassing going on. I knew all the clubs who would vote against, so there was no point in contacting them. It was the clubs who were a wee bit undecided that needed to be spoken to, and, if everyone voted the way they said they would, the result would fall in United for Change's favour.

The vote took place at around 2.30pm and was called at 12-9 in favour of backing United for Change. Jim Gardiner went berserk, calling it an absolute disgrace and stormed out of the pub. He was followed by Jimmy Jardine, taking it more in his stride, who came across to me and said, 'You knew the result before the vote, didn't you?' I nodded to Jimmy and he left with a wry smile on his face, I think in ironic admiration of the way it had been achieved. It was my belief that the two of them, particularly Jim Gardiner, thought it was a foregone conclusion that the motion would be defeated. The lesson for them was, 'Failing to prepare is preparing to fail.'

The decision did not sit well with Jim Gardiner at all. He could no longer back the status quo with the full support of the federation, only a minority. After that he did not take part in any of the meetings with the steering group or the club, taking more and more of a back seat. During that season he indicated that he would likely stand down as secretary at the AGM in June. That being the case, Shuggy and I set about finding a suitable replacement. That man would be Andy Woodrow from the Glenrothes Arabs, a very genial and capable guy, who agreed to stand when the AGM came round.

While all this had been going on, I had become really good friends with Mike Watson, Neil Glen and Derek Robertson and had formed a very good relationship with Eddie Thompson, keeping him up to date with all the information from the federation. In his quest to take over Eddie would often phone me to ask what was going on and obstacles to look out for.

At the 1999 federation AGM, Mike Barile, a staunch supporter of Jim McLean, decided to stand against me for the position of vice-chairman. He failed. When it came to voting on the secretary's position, I nominated Andy Woodrow, but Jim Gardiner sheepishly attempted to change his mind about standing at the last minute. I reminded him of publicly stating at a committee meeting he intended to stand down and it would now be unfair on Andy if that were not to be the case. He withdrew.

I remember Derek Robertson coming over to me after the meeting to congratulate me on the way I had managed to squeeze Jim Gardiner out of the equation. Shuggy Falconer was also voted on to the committee that year. It was all coming together as these appointments were to the benefit of United for Change and Eddie Thompson in particular.

I was a man who had slammed the politics within the refereeing movement and was now becoming as big a politician as Mike Watson and Neil Glen.

At the end of that season United finished second bottom, only six points ahead of relegated Dunfermline. There was no improvement at all, and all the glory European nights seemed like a hundred years ago. A month before the vote, Tommy McLean had been replaced as manager with United legend Paul 'Luggy' Sturrock taking up the reins. Although he worked his socks off, he couldn't turn things around either.

The next season was no better, United finished third bottom with one point fewer achieved than the previous campaign. Incidentally, Aberdeen finished bottom of the league that year but were not relegated as Falkirk, who had won the First Division, did not have a stadium which met with the SPL requirements.

While the Tangerines and their fans were having a torrid time of it, United for Change continued to meet on a regular basis to put pressure on Jim McLean to finally concede that his time with the club was coming to an end.

Since retiring as team boss, Wee Jim had appointed four managers, none of whom would give two years' service to the club. This had a massive effect on the field as managers and coaches had different ideas on how to play the game and the players required to fulfil their plans. There was no continuity whatsoever.

There was a section of the support who blamed United for Change for the unsettling effect we were allegedly having on the club and McLean in particular. Well, I am sorry guys, but we did not appoint the managers or pick the team and were therefore justified in our attempts to get new blood into the club.

Wee Jim continued to robustly reject any bids from Eddie Thompson to take over United and was becoming increasingly aggressive towards him, either through the media or on a personal basis. They both lived in the Dundee suburb of Broughty Ferry and would occasionally have to pass one another on the street. I was told Jim would walk right up into the millionaire grocer's face, stare him out and mouth all sorts of obscenities at him, even when grandchildren were present. This was totally unacceptable behaviour but was typical of Wee Jim when he wanted to display the despicable side of his character.

However, that said, Jim also had a very caring side to his personality. The A90 Arabs lost one of its members on Boxing Day 1996. Bert Thoms was only 46 years old when he died of a massive heart attack at his home in Westhill on the outskirts of Aberdeen. His two sons, Derek and Steven, were also members of our supporters' club and travelled regularly on the coach, although Derek was now living and working in Australia.

Bert's wife wrote to Wee Jim personally, telling him about her husband's love of United and how much he had enjoyed the successes of the 1980s and the recent Scottish Cup win against Rangers. She also informed him that Derek was returning home permanently from Australia and asked if it would be okay for him to use his dad's season ticket until the end of that season. Jim wrote a lovely letter in response saying how sorry he was to hear of Bert's passing and, of course, it would be fine for his ticket to be used by Derek.

Bert, of course, was originally from Dundee and had a lot of family and friends there. His funeral was held in Aberdeen on Hogmanay then early in the new year a memorial service was held in the City of Discovery. Mrs Thoms had placed a notice in the *Dundee Courier* newspaper letting everyone know of the venue, date and time when, lo and behold, who turned up totally unannounced to pay his respects but Jim McLean. He had obviously read the intimation, went out of his way not to make a big show of his presence and was thanked by the family for being there. That was the compassionate Wee Jim. Everybody who knew him accepted that he was very much a Jekyll and Hyde character.

In August 2000, very experienced campaigner Alex Smith, who had won the Scottish Cup with St Mirren and Aberdeen, was appointed manager by McLean to restore the fortunes of the club. Two months later Wee Jim would be forced to resign as chairman and director after that assault on BBC man John Barnes, so as not to incur the wrath of the SFA as well as a hefty fine and ban. He did, however, remain the majority shareholder.

There was still no improvement on the park either, with United again finishing second bottom of the league, a meagre five points ahead of St Mirren. With McLean no longer officially active within the club, it was felt that his resistance to Eddie's persistent quest to buy him out was now beginning to diminish. Further United for Change rallies were held and there was now a large appetite among the fans for a change in ownership to take the club in a new and more successful direction.

However, it would take over a year for Eddie Thompson to eventually become the owner of Dundee United. After yet another bottom-six finish in the league in 2002, Wee Jim sold out to Eddie in September of that year for an undisclosed sum. I had by this time resigned as vice-chairman of the federation, still being active with United for Change and, along with Shuggy Falconer, had become quite close friends with Eddie as well as the other guys within the pressure group. Shug had by now become chairman of the federation, a very sensible and popular choice with the fans.

After a couple of weeks in charge the first big decision for Eddie Thompson to make under his ownership was to sack manager Alex Smith and replace him temporarily with first team coach Paul Hegarty, another United legend and former captain. Eddie and Paul had become very close friends over the years, in fact he had been chairman of Heggie's testimonial committee a few years earlier.

However, the appointment was temporary and Eddie's top target to take over was Ian McCall, who was doing extremely well with First Division side Falkirk and had a good track record at that level. After a lot of soul-searching, pressure from his board of directors and a good pay rise, McCall turned down United's offer. Hegarty would continue in temporary charge, at least for another few months.

The chairman had now turned his attention to another manager in the First Division, a man I knew very well from my spell living in Elgin and refereeing in the Highland League, Inverness Caley Thistle's Steve Paterson. 'Pele', as he was known locally as a youngster and throughout his career, hailed from the Moray village of Fochabers and after spending a short time at Highland League Nairn County, moved south to join Manchester United.

He spent five years at Old Trafford before moving to Sheffield United, where he sustained a career-threatening injury in a pre-season friendly. Pele eventually accepted an insurance pay-out, meaning he could never play top-flight football in England again. He returned briefly to the Highlands to turn out for Buckie Thistle, before spells in Hong Kong, Australia and Japan.

Pele returned to his homeland for a second time in the late 1980s and spent two years managing Elgin City, winning the Highland League, Scottish Qualifying Cup (North) and the Highland League Cup twice. He then moved to Huntly where he was even more successful with two Highland League titles, Qualifying Cup, Highland League Cup and Aberdeenshire Cup in a five-year stint before moving to Inverness.

Eddie Thompson was very much aware that I knew Pele very well and sounded me out about him. I gave the chairman as much information as I could and having looked at his overall managerial record, wanted to make an approach for him. In the world of football everything is not totally done 'by the book' and Eddie should have contacted the Inverness club first. Why do that? He needed to know if Pele was interested in the post before contacting his employers.

Eddie asked me if I had a phone number for Pele. Now, despite the fact I knew him well, we were not best pals and although I did not have a contact number for him, I knew a man who would – my old pal Willie Grant, who was by now the Highland League football correspondent for the *Sunday Post* and lived in the same village of Garmouth. Steve had always looked up to Willie and during their years of friendship sought his counsel on many occasions.

I contacted Willie, who was sworn to secrecy along with yours truly, and passed Pele's phone number on to Eddie Thompson. In fairness to the chairman, as he always did with people close to him, he kept me informed as to how negotiations were progressing.

Prior to travelling down to Rugby Park to face Kilmarnock on the first Saturday in November, Shuggy and I had been informed by Eddie that Pele was to be unveiled as United's new manager on the Monday afternoon. The rest of the guys on the coach knew there was something afoot, but we said nothing.

Ironically, United won 2-1 with goals from Steven Thompson and Jim McIntyre, which was Hegarty's first league success in charge of the team. As the happy bunch of Arabs journeyed our way back north, I received a call on my mobile from a journalist friend of mine, who was well informed of what was going on, giving me some astonishing news. 'Gunner,' he said, 'it's not happening, I don't know what the circumstances are, but Paterson will not be your new manager.'

Shug and I were dumbfounded. What on earth had gone wrong? On the Monday there was a war of words between Inverness and United with claims and counter claims which did neither club any favours as there were a few inaccuracies coming out from both.

As it turned out, I was informed it was for sound personal reasons that Steve Paterson could not accept the post of manager at Tannadice. As they were personal to Pele I am not going to go into the details.

Eddie was getting a rough ride in his first few months in charge, but events were to change after the turn of the year. Without a win in ten weeks, the chairman took the decision to dismiss Paul Hegarty at the end of January and eventually landed his initial target in Ian McCall. Falkirk were runaway leaders in the First Division, but because their Brockville ground still did not meet the criteria laid down by the SPL, were unlikely to get promoted for the second time in three years. United finished second bottom of the league again that season, but the new manager surely had to be given time.

The 2003/04 season proved to be a vast improvement, and although United did not fare well in the domestic cup competitions, they finished a creditable fifth in the league, which was their first top-six slot for seven years. McCall looked like he was becoming the real deal and formed a close relationship with the chairman and fans alike. I remember having some great trips with the A90 Arabs that season, regardless of the results.

Eddie Thompson was now beginning to forge excellent relationships with the United support because of his open and transparent personality, meeting regularly with the federation, the newly formed Arab Trust, which was to eventually become the second largest shareholder within Dundee United, and the general fanbase at large. This was in complete contrast to the previous regime who had very much a siege mentality.

However, there was one major worry facing the club. Eddie had been diagnosed with prostate cancer in 2003. His consultant gave him a choice between having surgery or treatment to get rid of the disease. Choosing to go down the route of being operated on he had a better chance of a complete recovery, but that would have meant a long period of recuperation away from Tannadice, a decision he could not contemplate as he needed to be present on a daily basis to be able to lift the fortunes of his beloved United. He chose to take the treatment option with the knowledge that he was taking a risk. He literally gambled with his life for the sake of the club.

When Eddie bought Jim McLean's shares, he appointed Derek Robertson as one of his directors. It was a shrewd move on his part as Derek was a died-in-the-wool Arab, a very intelligent, forward-thinking man and a tireless worker on behalf of the club, despite having to cope with the illness ME, otherwise known as Chronic Fatigue Syndrome. He was also a great guy and very good friend to all at Tannadice. The combination of those two men helped build a very close relationship between the club and the fans.

Now and again Eddie would invite Shug and I into the boardroom at a few games to enjoy the club's hospitality, where we met a few interesting people along the way. Senior members of the A90 Arabs were convinced the only reason the chairman invited us was when the OVD rum in the boardroom was going out of date and we were commissioned to demolish it!

One of the football men we came across was a former German international with over 50 caps for his country, Rainer Bonhof. He was manager of the Scotland under-21 squad at the time when compatriot Berti Vogts was in charge of the senior team. His views on the game, and how it should be played, were quite different from what Shug and I were used to and we both found it very interesting and refreshing.

In another visit United were playing Aberdeen, their great rivals from the Granite City. Shug and I took our seats in the box reserved for directors and guests at that time immediately behind the dugouts (now known as The Captain's Table which is used for hospitality purposes). There was a fair bit of space in our section as Eddie and some of the others preferred to sit in the upper section of the East Stand behind the goal. The Aberdeen section was full. A few minutes into the game I heard a familiar voice behind me. It was Wee Jim chatting to some of the Dons' officials. He moved as if to find a seat in our section, but when he saw Shuggy and I, he stopped in his tracks and proceeded to stand behind the Aberdeen contingent for the remainder of the first half. Why did he have to behave like that? We would have made him more than welcome. Just because we disagreed at the way he had run the club as chairman did not mean to say that we had forgotten the previous glories he brought as manager. For that we will forever be grateful. He either found another seat for the second half or just left.

Despite the progress made the previous season, 2004/05 provided yet another relegation battle for United, although they did reach the semi-final of the

League Cup and the Scottish Cup Final. Too many draws in the league and a 7-1 thrashing from Rangers in the League Cup semi were to prove McCall's downfall. Qualifying for the Scottish Cup semi-final with a 4-1 drubbing of Aberdeen a couple of weeks previously was not enough to save him, and Eddie dispensed with his services in March. Ian's assistant, Gordon Chisholm, was placed in temporary charge.

United finished ninth in the league, a paltry three points ahead of our neighbours from down the road who were relegated. They did atone slightly, with a sterling performance in the final against Celtic. Although having most of the possession, albeit with less chances, the Tangerines went down 1-0 to an early deflected Alan Thompson free kick.

During the week leading up to the cup final, Chisholm was given the manager's job on a permanent basis by Eddie, a decision which many fans thought, including myself, was quite rash as the man had not proved himself at that level at all. If he had waited until after the final, Eddie would have had the whole summer to look for the most suitable candidate. He was just so desperate for success, but his deep love for the club perhaps led to him making snap judgements on major issues.

United's fortunes did not improve any under Chisholm's tenure and with only five league victories and first-time exits in both cup competitions he was sacked in January 2006. His replacement was the 1994 Scottish Cup-winning hero, a local lad and fan, Craig Brewster, who was doing well with Caley Thistle up in Inverness. His appointment was very popular with the fans, but would it be the right one? Only time would tell.

In the remaining league campaign of that season with Brewster at the helm, United only won once in 16 matches. Hardly the kind of form that heroes were made of.

As the next season got under way it was becoming increasingly obvious that Brewster, despite his ability on the park and legendary status with the fans, was not the man for the job. Thompson was very aware of the situation and was now taking his time to cast his eyes far and wide to find a replacement who would finally turn things round for the club. He knew he had made mistakes and had to get United out of this predicament once and for all.

With only one win in his first ten matches of the campaign, Brewster travelled with his troops up to Aberdeen, where United surrendered tamely in a 3-1 defeat. His post-match press conference was pathetic by any standards. He virtually wrote his own resignation letter with a statement saying he felt he could not turn things around and didn't know what to do next.

One excellent piece of business completed by the club on Brewster's arrival was the appointment of Steve Campbell, who had worked with him up at Inverness, initially as under-19 coach. Steve had fantastic knowledge of youth football around the Tayside area and beyond. He discovered many a young talent who went on to represent United well, before moving on to bigger clubs at home and abroad. It was no surprise when Campbell was appointed youth director in 2009.

It was the popular consensus of opinion that Eddie now had only a week to get a new man in. Quite a few names had been bandied about, but there was one in particular which stood out above all the rest. It was the last chance saloon for the chairman to get it right before the natives got extremely restless. All would be revealed the Monday following Brewster's last game in charge, ironically a 5-1 thrashing away to Falkirk. Absolutely humiliating for any Arab to take.

A funny wee story for you just before I talk about Craig Levein. I was working in the motor trade for a car warranty company at that time, and part of the geographical territory I had to cover was the Kingdom of Fife, which I travelled to every Monday morning. One of the dealers I visited was based in Crossgates just outside Dunfermline. Jim was a big football fan, a season ticket holder at East End Park, home of Dunfermline Athletic. I arrived at his base around 10.30am on the Monday after that debacle at Falkirk and big Jim was letting me know about it, big style. Dunfermline were also looking for a new manager, with Pars legend Jim Leishman moving the previous week from the dug-out to a position upstairs as general manager.

Jim knew about my previous involvement with United for Change and that I was also a personal friend of Eddie Thompson. On that morning he seemed to be quite excited that Dunfermline were on the verge of appointing a new boss. He had been informed the day before by a close friend who had 'contacts within the club' at East End Park, that former Hearts gaffer Craig Levein would be that man. He went white when he saw the wry smile on my face and I winked at him, asking whether he was absolutely sure.

Jim went bananas. 'You know different?' he roared. 'You know something, you always know what's going

on at your club? Levein's going to Tannadice, isn't he?'
I neither confirmed nor denied his observation, but
did ask him to keep his radio on after lunchtime. He
was so incensed he immediately phoned his 'contact'
and proceeded to give the guy a right good rollicking
about giving him duff information, without actually
giving out any clues about why he knew different or
where Craig Levein might be going. That was Jim's
revenge on his mate.

Levein was managing his boyhood heroes Raith
Rovers, albeit on a non-contract basis, allowing him
to move on freely if a bigger club came in for him.
He was unveiled at a press conference at Tannadice
that Monday afternoon. Craig came with an excellent
track record – three years cutting his teeth in the lower
leagues as boss of Cowdenbeath and four years at
Tynecastle where he was the first man since the 1960s
to take Hearts on two successive European campaigns
with third place finishes in the league. He also spent
around 18 months in the English Championship with
Leicester City where he was not very well supported by
his board, never being given any money to spend on
players to improve his squad.

Levein took trusted lieutenant, Peter Houston, from
his spells at Tynecastle and Leicester, as his assistant

manager and this proved to be the recipe for success over the next few years.

It was then widely known that Eddie Thompson's cancer was terminal. Regular treatment and steroids giving him a prolonged and decent quality of life. He continued to work tirelessly as chairman of United and formed a close and excellent working relationship with Craig.

The new manager immediately endeared himself to the United faithful with a 2-1 success at home to Rangers. They won six and drew one of their next ten games before the turn of the year. Things were looking up. However, a poor second half of the season yielded ninth position for the fourth year in a row.

Levein's first full season in charge was to prove a turning point in the fortunes of the club. Thompson also promoted him to the board in January 2008 as director of football. United finished fifth in the league, only their second top-six berth in 11 years. They also reached the final of the League Cup in March, undeservedly losing out to Rangers in a penalty shoot-out after a 2-2 draw. Noel Hunt had opened the Tangerines' account ten minutes before half-time, when early in the second half United's Scandinavian full-back, Christian Kalvenes, was crudely upended by Rangers' Spanish defender Carlos Cuellar inside the penalty area right in front of where Shug and I were sitting. Referee Kenny Clark wrongly waved play on, yet another decision which went against the team on big occasions at Hampden. I firmly believe if a penalty had been correctly awarded, and converted, United would have gone on to win the game quite comfortably.

As it happened, the Ibrox side luckily equalised with five minutes to go, as young Mark Kerr inexplicably played the ball across his own penalty area for keeper Zaluska to clear upfield, but Kris Boyd nipped in to score, taking the match to extra time. The Tangerines again took the lead through Mark De Vries, only for Boyd again to equalise. United lost 3-2 on penalties.

It was heartbreaking. I particularly felt for Eddie, who by now was quite ill, but did attend the game. He had worked so hard for the club, ploughing in a few million pounds of his own fortune to bring success. My abiding memory of the match was a shot of Eddie on the big screen at Hampden, with the score at 2-1, roaring his team on and encouraging the fans to do likewise. It would have brought a tear to a glass eye. Most of the fans wore tangerine T-shirts with 'There's

Only One Eddie Thompson' emblazoned on the front and on the back Eddie's famous quote:

'You can change your wife, your house, your car, but you can never change your team. Chairmen come and go, boards come and go, but the fans remain. They are the one true constant. I've just been a custodian of the club.'

Spoken like the true leader he was with a deep love for his football team.

At the beginning of the next season Eddie's health was deteriorating quickly and he now needed a wheelchair to assist him to get around. United's first home game was against Celtic and, as he was wheeled up the track in front of the away support to sit near the dugout, the rapturous applause he received from the Hoops' faithful was a magnificent gesture by them.

Eddie passed away peacefully in Ninewells Hospital, Dundee, on 15 October 2008. He had been in charge at Tannadice for six years and during that spell he had ploughed in millions of his own money for the benefit of the club. After a shaky first few years, with the management team of Craig Levein and Peter Houston now at the helm, the team's fortunes were beginning to change at last and now the main man was gone.

On another visit to the boardroom earlier that year, Eddie had informed Shug and I that when he sold his convenience store chain in 2004 he had, as any father would, given his daughter Justine and son Stephen, both loyal United fans, a sum of money from the proceeds. Justine had invested her money wisely and made a good few quid on stocks and shares, the chairman advised us proudly. His son – well, let's just say he didn't follow in his sister's footsteps. Eddie, knowing he was on borrowed time, was indicating to us that he would have preferred Justine to take control of United when he was no longer around.

Tragically, this would never happen. Just three days before Eddie died, Justine's husband, Ken Mitchell, was killed in a horrific motorcycle accident travelling from Edinburgh. She witnessed him lose control from the rear-view mirror of her car which was just in front. Ironically, the couple had been on their way to Ninewells to say their final goodbyes to Eddie.

With their one-year-old son Monty to bring up on her own, there was no way Justine could combine family life with running a football club, coupled with the fact she had just lost her husband and father only days apart. She couldn't bear to come to Tannadice for over a year after that.

So her brother took over as chairman the day after Eddie's death and all I will say at this juncture is he was absolutely nothing like his father.

The funeral in Broughty Ferry was by invitation only and all organised by the man himself. He booked coaches to take mourners from Tannadice to the church and selected the musical pieces to be played. Craig Levein broke down as he paid a fitting tribute to his chairman and very close friend. Fans lined the streets to pay their respects to 'one of their own'. Afterwards, the coaches returned to the ground for refreshments and everyone shared their own personal memories of Eddie Thompson.

17

ANOTHER TROPHY

THE TEAM continued to flourish, finishing fifth in the league and reaching the semi-final of the League Cup, losing out to Celtic in a tense penalty shoot-out in January 2009. This was the best shape the club had been in for years.

The 2009/10 season holds bittersweet memories for me. United had only lost two league games up until mid-December and during that spell Levein's name was being touted for a variety of managerial posts. The Scottish FA had recently sacked national team manager George Burley when it approached the club to ask to speak to Craig. It was widely known to the footballing public what was going on and I thought to myself that being only 45 he was far too young to take on that role. In my opinion it was a position for a man towards the end of his career having achieved a fair amount of success at club level.

The United fans did not want Craig to leave. He was an excellent manager, the best we had since the heady days of Wee Jim, and on the cusp of achieving great things at Tannadice. In the end the pull of managing his country was too much for him to miss out on, but my thoughts were that by taking on the Scotland job, if things didn't work out it could destroy his entire career. They didn't and it did.

Peter Houston was placed in temporary charge of the team on Levein's departure two days before Christmas. After a deal to bring Pat Fenlon from Ireland fell apart, he was appointed on a permanent basis until the end of the season in late January.

An excellent run from then until the end of the season saw the club finish third in the league and reach the Scottish Cup Final against Ross County. It was a fantastic day out at the national stadium in the sunshine as United ran out comfortable 3-0 winners. Although he was no longer with us that was the trophy Eddie Thompson deserved.

For his efforts, Houston was rewarded with a three-year contract. He continued the excellent work of his old gaffer by finishing fourth in the league and reaching both the quarter-final of the Scottish and League Cups in successive seasons. This also ensured a slot in the Europa League qualifiers for a third year in a row.

Houston had by now proved himself as a manager in his own right, having spent a few years as a number two. I liked him. He was a very good coach who knew how to man-manage his players and, most importantly, got results.

After a decent, but unspectacular, first half of the 2012/13 season, Stephen Thompson indicated he would like to extend the manager's contract, but inexplicably wanted him to take a cut in wages. Here was a man who had the best record at Tannadice since Jim McLean, along with winning the Scottish Cup, and Thompson wanted to reduce his salary. His father must have turned in his grave. He would have done the opposite and given Peter a deserved bonus.

During his time in charge, he had introduced a few good youngsters into the team, such as Stuart Armstrong, Gary Mackay-Steven, Scott Allan, John Souttar and Ryan Gauld. The future looked very bright indeed for the club. Peter took a little bit of time to ponder over his chairman's derisory offer and announced on 17 January that he would leave United at the end of the season. Incidentally, three days earlier, Blackpool had been given permission by Thompson to speak to Houston about their managerial vacancy, although nothing came of it. Dundee United and Peter Houston parted company on 28 January 2013 by 'mutual consent'. In my view, Stephen Thompson had all but pushed his manager out of the door, making the biggest mistake of his tenure so far. There would be many more to follow.

18

THE BEGINNING
OF THE DECLINE

IT APPEARED from the outside that Stephen Thompson had been actively looking for a new manager while Peter Houston was still employed by the club. Peter's seat in his office was still warm when Partick Thistle boss Jackie McNamara was appointed as his successor only two days after leaving. Others had been interviewed, including former player Derek McInnes, who was out of work after leaving Bristol City. McInnes was my first choice as he had done a good job at St Johnstone before going south, but like many Scottish managers, wasn't given a proper chance in England.

I mentioned McInnes to United director and good friend, Derek Robertson, who told me that he had made a mess of his interview by coming across as quite arrogant. I was very surprised and disappointed to hear that as I thought McInnes was quite an intelligent, level-headed guy. Jackie McNamara's arrival on Tannadice Street didn't exactly set the heather on fire, United scraping into the top six courtesy of a last-minute winner against Aberdeen at home. They went on to win only one of their remaining five games. United did reach the semi- final of the Scottish Cup, losing out 4-3 after extra time in an epic encounter against Celtic.

McNamara made a number of new signings in the close season, notably Nadir Ciftci, Paul Paton and Andy Robertson, now of Liverpool and Scotland fame. United had a successful season, finishing fourth in the league and losing 2-0 to St Johnstone in the Scottish Cup Final.

Despite having a very good start to the 2014/15 season with 13 wins prior to facing Aberdeen in the Scottish League Cup semi-final at the end of January, there didn't seem to be much fluency to United's play, scraping wins by the skin of their teeth, apart from hammering rivals Dundee twice, 4-1 and 6-2 respectively. Another problem appeared to be a lack of discipline.

The Tangerines defeated Aberdeen 2-1 in that semi-final and were due to face Celtic in the final in

March. However, what happened off the field would make the headlines on the following Monday – transfer deadline day.

Gary Mackay-Steven was out of contract at the end of the season and had already signed a pre-contract agreement to join Celtic in the summer. Robertson, after one excellent season, had already been sold to Hull City for £2.85m in July the previous year. On deadline day the news had filtered through that Stuart Armstrong was to join Celtic for £1.6m with Mackay- Steven also leaving immediately for a fee of £250,000. This was seen by the United faithful as a massive betrayal by Stephen Thompson. They were due to meet Celtic in the League Cup Final in less than two months without two of their best players, whowould instead sit in the stand as spectators because they would not be eligible to play for their new club having been cup-tied by the Tangerines. I felt this was another blunder by the chairman, who claimed that Armstrong had requested the move. Stuart has always strongly denied that story.

In another revelation in the media, it was disclosed that Jackie McNamara and his management team received a percentage of the transfer fee from any player they had developed. This was not an uncommon practice in England, particularly in the lower leagues, where managers would accept lower salaries to be topped up by any transfer cash coming into their clubs. However, it was virtually unheard of in Scotland and this incensed the United fans who viewed it as a conflict of interest on the part of McNamara. How did the press get a hold of this information? Some speculated thatThompson had leaked it out from the club in order to deflect the flak away from himself.

United fans were now beginning to get restless, wondering what was going on at boardroom level. Things had never been the same since Eddie had gone. He was open and honest with the supporters, always passing on non-confidential information. His son was a different animal, dour and secretive, and it was hard to know what he was thinking. The management team became a target for the fans, because of the deal on transfers they had made with Thompson when signing up at Tannadice. A chasm was now beginning to appear between the club and its faithful followers. Thankfully, Stevie Campbell was there to steady the ship and continue to develop the young talent coming through the ranks. Although his title was director of youth, he took his place in the first team dugout every week as quite a few of the first-team squad had got there because of his knowledge and guidance. His presence gave them confidence and helped them concentrate on the job ahead.

Dundee United played four competitive domestic matches in March that season, all against the same club – Celtic.

They faced the Hoops once in the league, twice in the Scottish Cup (one a replay after a 1-1 draw at Tannadice) and in the League Cup Final. That kind of scenario was all too familiar in the goldfish bowl of Scottish football.

The Tangerines lost the cup final 2-0 but surrendered with a mere whimper, creating very few chances during the 90 minutes. Although a fourth-place finish looked like a decent league campaign, United only had a plus-two goal difference, leaking 56 goals in the process. Things were going downhill, and fast.

The next season had barely started when the fans were hit with a bombshell – Stevie Campbell had been suspended on full pay by Stephen Thompson pending an investigation for gross misconduct. It was a huge shock to the United faithful, who couldn't quite believe that Campbell and the words 'gross misconduct' appeared in the same sentence. What on earth was going on?

Fans were left dumbfounded.

It seems nobody will never know the truth surrounding his eventual departure from Dundee United. Stevie intended to take the club to an industrial tribunal. However, before this was due to take place, he resigned his post in November 2016 after agreeing a deal with Thompson. It is likely it included what is commonly known in Dundee as a 'shut yir puss' clause (translated as 'not allowed to publicly reveal any details of the arrangement and reasons why').

It was rumoured that Campbell had become increasingly concerned about the lack of fitness of the players and the attitude of the management team towards their duties. He had already been banished from the first-team bench.

Ironically, after a very poor start to the season and a lot of pressure from the fans, McNamara and his coaching team were sacked at the end of September following a defeat to St Johnstone in Perth, well before Campbell's eventual departure.

Ex-United hero and Finnish international player and manager, Mixu Paatelainen, was appointed to take charge of team affairs three weeks later, but it looked like an impossible task as the team was in a rapid downward spiral.

After only eight wins all season, United were relegated to the Championship, as it is now known, and Mixu was relieved of his duties after only seven months in charge. Absolute devastation for all Arabs, and to add insult to injury, city rivals Dundee FC were the team to officially put the club down with a 2-1 victory at Dens Park.

19

LIFE IN THE CHAMPIONSHIP

AS DUNDEE United's first season in the Championship began, former midfielder Ray McKinnon was drafted in by Stephen Thompson to take charge of team affairs. Ray had been a highly respected coach at the SFA, before moving on to successful spells managing Brechin City and Raith Rovers. It was a strange experience for the fans as they would not now be facing Celtic, Rangers, Aberdeen and the rest, but travelling to places such as Greenock, Dumbarton and Dumfries – such are the ups and downs of supporting a provincial Scottish club.

The team had a good start to the season and by Christmas were top of the league, just ahead of Hibernian, who were the bookies' favourites for the title. However, a shocking run of only four wins between Hogmanay and the end of the term saw United come third behind the Edinburgh side and Falkirk. That was nowhere near good enough for a club of United's standing. Their inability to beat sides at the bottom end of the table cost the Tangerines dearly. Dumbarton, Raith and Ayr, who finished in the bottom three, took a total of 17 points from them. If that had been turned around it would have been enough to win the title by three points.

It was then into the complicated play-offs. In the Championship it was different from Leagues 1 and 2. Fourth top played third top, the winners played second top and the victors from that game played the team who finished second bottom in the Premiership. This system was geared to give the advantage to the bigger league team, as they would only have to play one home and away tie, as opposed to three for the teams who finished third or fourth top should they progress.

A comfortable 5-1 aggregate win against Morton meant United would meet Falkirk next. A 2-2 draw at home provided a tricky visit to the Falkirk Stadium, however, a late and very rare Paul Dixon header saw them overcome the Bairns 2-1. The final was against the perennial survivors of many Premiership relegation battles, Hamilton Academical. The first leg at home finished 0-0 but was shrouded in controversy. United's striker, local lad Simon Murray, who had been booked in the first half, was brought down inside the penalty area by a Hamilton defender with less than 15 minutes to play. Instead of pointing to the spot, referee Steven McLean awarded an indirect free kick to Hamilton and booked Murray for diving, which meant he was sent off. Accies won the return leg 1-0, keeping United down for a further season.

Without a shadow of doubt, if that penalty had been correctly awarded and converted, the club would have returned to the top division at the first time of asking.

There were doubts among a section of the support that McKinnon was perhaps out of his depth managing his hometown club. He didn't appear to be able to change personnel or tactics when things were not going right on the park. Ray was a lovely guy and worked really hard, but many didn't think he was the man to take the club forward.

The next campaign started brightly enough with three successive victories, albeit by only one-goal margins. After successive defeats to Livingston and

Inverness in October, Stephen Thompson wielded the axe once more, sacking McKinnon after a home reverse to the Highlanders.

Thompson's running of the club was now being called into question. His commitment, in particular, was under very close scrutiny as he seemed to be more interested in trying to invest in Australian club Newcastle Jets than getting United out of the Championship. His personal life had regularly been the subject of media attention, he never seemed to be around Tannadice and constantly ignored pleas from the fans for a meeting to discuss what was going on and what the plans were for the future.

Then he made the most monumental of cock ups by appointing former Hearts manager Csaba Laszlo to take over from Ray McKinnon a couple of weeks after his departure. Laszlo didn't have a clue. Speaking very little English, the players and coaches could not understand him. How the hell were the team meant to perform on the field with that clown in charge? He used to run up and down the touchline, shouting and waving his arms all over the place, and the crowd could see the players clearly shrugging their shoulders and shaking their heads in total dismay at his antics.

Thompson hadcome under increasing pressure from the supporters to step down as chairman. At the beginning of March 2018 he meekly caved in and was replaced by highly respected former financial industry guru Mike Martin, who had recently acquired a 30 per cent shareholding in the club, and only a week earlier had purchased the youth training facility. Thompson also stated that he would sell the bulk of his shares within the next few months.

After that United's home form was decent, but their away record was disgraceful. On an away table only, they would have finished seventh. As it turned out at the end of the season the Arabs finished third, a point behind Livingston but 13 further back than champions St Mirren.

Play-off time again. After a 0-0 first leg at East End Park against Dunfermline, the return game ended 2-1 in United's favour.

Next up were Livingston at home, where the visitors took the lead after only two minutes. The home side restored parity only 60 seconds later and went into the lead just before the half-hour. They were totally dominant for almost the rest of the match until Livi scored two quick goals within three minutes, well against the run of play, to win 3-2. United had blown it again, drawing the return 1-1 and leaving their faithful fans devastated once more.

After an indifferent start to the next campaign, Laszlo was shown the door at the end of September immediately after a 5-1 home defeat at the hands of Ross County. He had been in charge for less than a year and it brought an end to a horrendous spell for the loyal support with results poor and performances even worse. During Laszlo's time at the helm, Shuggy and I reckoned we spent more time in the nearby Troll Inn on a Saturday afternoon than we did at Tannadice, it was that bad.

Former Hearts and MK Dons manager Robbie Neilson, who also played for the club under Peter Houston for a short spell, was placed in charge of team affairs a week after Laszlo's departure.

The club were under new ownership in December when American entrepreneur Mark Ogren bought an 85 per cent stake in Dundee United. He immediately pledged to supply cash to strengthen the team in the forthcoming January transfer window. I have always been quite suspicious of foreign football club owners, wondering what their long-term real agenda might be. However, from the off, Mr Ogren seemed to be genuine enough, stressing his immediate objective was to steer the club back to the Premiership and push on from there. What the fans really needed to know was whether there was any connection between him and his fellow countrymen who were in charge across the road at Dens Park. We were assured there wasn't, isn't and never will be. Good enough for me.

During the first few games of Neilson's reign, I felt that he was over-cautious in his style of play, the team not scoring nearly enough goals. However, sufficient points were gained to see them finish in second place, six points behind Ross County. Yet again, their failure to beat the bottom three clubs cost United dearly, losing ten points to Alloa, Queen of the South and relegated Falkirk.

The dreaded play-offs had to be faced once more. With a comfortable 4-0 aggregate win over Inverness, confidence was high in the camp that United would once more climb up to the top table of Scottish football. A dour 0-0 draw with St Mirren at Tannadice was followed by an equally tense affair at St Mirren Park. Nicky Clark opened the Arabs' account from the penalty spot on 23 minutes, only for the Paisley men to equalise shortly afterwards. The score remained the same after 90 minutes and then extra time. A nerve-wracking penalty shoot-out took place with St Mirren winning 2-0 after United had missed all four spot kicks they had taken. They had failed miserably, yet again, losing out to clubs who were much smaller than them. How much more could the Arabs' faithful take? I left St Mirren Park that day like a man demented. It took me until Wednesday to fully calm down, think to myself, it is what it is, and look forward to the next season as I had already purchased my season ticket a few weeks previously.

The new regime at boardroom level had been put in place at the beginning of the year. Mark Ogren's son Scott was also appointed to the board along with current directors David Dorward and Jimmy Fyfe. As Ogren would be based in the United States most of the time he had to build a good team to run the club in his absence. Former policeman and respected football agent Tony Asghar, who had worked with many top clubs in England, became sporting director, and former Derby County finance chief Mal Brannigan took up the role of managing director. With years of experience in business and football installed to run the club, the supporters were justified in feeling optimistic about the future.

Before the start of the 2019/20 season, Dundee United made the biggest signing in their recent history.

Lawrence Shankland had been playing for Ayr United for the last two seasons and was out of contract. He had scored a phenomenal 50 goals in 61 appearances during that spell and was hotly tipped to move to one of the Championship clubs in England. However, Tony Asghar's negotiating skills must have worked wonders on the Glasgwegian, coupled with the fact he was a free agent and there would be no transfer fee, as Lawrence decided it would be more beneficial to his career at that stage to join up at Tannadice on a three-year deal.

Although only 24 years of age, Shankland had a fair bit of experience behind him. He came through the youth ranks at Queen's Park before moving to Aberdeen in 2013. He spent four years at Pittodrie, making only 17 first-team appearances without scoring, and had loan spells at Dunfermline, St Mirren and Morton before joining up with Ian McCall at Ayr.

The board had shown great ambition in bringing this young man to the club. He would have been given a sizeable signing-on fee to become the highest-paid player in the squad. Other new additions were Shankland's team-mate at Somerset Park, Liam Smith, along with Dillon Powers, Peter Pawlett, Adrian Sporle and Ian Harkes, son of former USA international

John. The 20-year-old Louis Appere, who had been farmed out the previous season to Junior side Broughty Athletic, also came into the first-team pool.

United were certainly going for it. They just HAD to get promoted at the end of the season and the fans were demanding it.

They got off to a fantastic start to the league campaign, winning the first four games, including a 6-2 rout of neighbours Dundee who had been relegated the previous season. Shankland was proving his worth by scoring seven of the 14 goals United notched.

After losing three out of the next five matches, the Arabs went on a 13-game unbeaten run until February, dropping only four points in the process. At one point they were 24 points ahead of their nearest rivals at the top of the league table. 'Pump it, pump it, pump it up, United's going up!' was the cry of the Tannadice faithful.

As usually happens during a season, a wee dip in form saw the team drop 12 points out of the next 18 available.

And then.

20

CORONAVIRUS OF 2020

WHEN I started to pen my football memories in the summer of 2019, I gave myself two years to complete the project as I could only commit to writing it on my Friday day off from work and the odd session of an evening or at the weekend. The reason I had every Friday off was that I was working the same hours as previously but condensing them over four days instead of five.

However, as we will all recall, the biggest pandemic to hit our planet since Spanish flu after World War One rained down on the UK in March 2020 – coronavirus, or COVID-19 as it was also known. This meant a complete lockdown for the whole country, where we were all confined to our homes, only allowed out for essential shopping and daily exercise, and had to keep a distance of two metres from any other person outside of your own house.

To begin with I was working from home, but as my client base within the advertising industry was in the travel and entertainment worlds, there was no business to be had and eventually my colleagues and I were furloughed. This was a scheme adopted by the government where they paid 80 per cent of your salary and I was fortunate enough that my employers made up the other 20 per cent. This was a way of making sure that jobs were safe and nationwide redundancies were avoided.

Unprecedented times, but it gave me the time and opportunity to work on this book and I set myself a new deadline for publication of late 2020.

The football world in Scotland and beyond was turned upside down with the SFA suspending all levels of the game from 14 March for an indefinite period. This was going to affect the smaller clubs more than those in the top tier and it was feared some would go out of business altogether as the largest part of their income came from fans paying at the gate.

The biggest question for Dundee United fans was what would happen next. The team was sitting at the top of the Championship, 14 points clear of second-placed Inverness, being 23 goals better off, and there were still eight games to play. Mathematically, United could have been caught by the Highlanders, but it was highly unlikely. Would the season restart, be declared null and void or stopped with current league positions counting for promotion and relegation purposes?

The Scottish Professional Football League (SPFL) board, after many discussions in online virtual meetings because of social distancing rules, decided that their member clubs would vote on whether to end the season (final positions being given on an average points per game basis) in the three lower divisions but defer any decision on the Premiership. It was also decided by the ruling body that to write the season off was out of the question as nearly 80 per cent of the fixtures had been completed.

The vote was a very complicated affair. Some 75 per cent of the clubs in each division would have to vote in favour of the motion for it to be carried, which meant nine clubs in the Premiership and eight in each of the other three divisions. All clubs would receive ballot papers by e-mail and after casting their vote would return them to the SPFL in the same way.

In the Premiership, where Rangers and Hearts voted against the proposal, and Leagues 1 and 2 the 75 per cent threshold was easily achieved. In the

Championship nine out of the ten clubs' votes had been received by the governing body, with Inverness and Partick Thistle voting against. The only club still to vote were Dundee and it had been strongly rumoured that they would also vote no. If that were to be the case, the motion would have been defeated.

Dundee claimed they had sent in their ballot paper by e-mail in time for the 5pm deadline on Friday, 10 April and had, indeed, voted against the proposals. The SPFL were adamant that it had not arrived at their Hampden Park headquarters. It had all become a bit of a farce as a couple of days passed and Dundee's vote had still not been received. There were claims by certain clubs that there had been a bit of skulduggery going on within the ruling body. By Wednesday, Dundee's chairman John Nelms had a change of heart and finally e-mailed their decision in favour of officially ending the season for lower league clubs.

Dundee United were champions and back in the big time. Raith Rovers and Cove Rangers, from Leagues 1 and 2 respectively, were also promoted. Partick Thistle and Stranraer were relegated from their divisions and there was to be no play-off between the bottom team in League 2 and the winner of the Highland and Lowland leagues contest.

The way the whole episode had been handled was heavily criticised within the media and created a war of words between some clubs and the SPFL. Rangers were at the forefront of the protests, which seemed strange as they really had nothing at stake. They were 13 points behind Celtic in the Premiership with only nine games left to play. Although they had a game in hand over their city rivals and mathematically could have overtaken them, it would have been very unlikely, impossible even, had the Premiership season been continued.

The Ibrox club then called for a full independent investigation into the proceedings of the voting process, claiming some clubs had been bullied into voting in the SPFL's favour. They also wanted the ruling body's chief executive Neil Doncaster, and lawyer Rod McKenzie, suspended immediately.

Chartered accountancy giants Deloitte were hired by the SPFL to carry out a full forensic independent investigation and they found no evidence of any improper behaviour. This did not, however, satisfy Rangers, who called the outcome 'too narrow' and said it was 'not addressing the wider issues of the manner in which the SPFL was being run'.

Football authorities the world over are always open to criticism and their top personnel will become targets of abuse from clubs and media alike. However, this was an unprecedented time for everyone with thousands of deaths worldwide at the hands of the pandemic, and a bit of common sense and humanity should have prevailed.

It was now becoming increasingly unlikely that the Scottish Premiership season could be completed within an acceptable time frame, as the country was still in lockdown. After a meeting of the clubs on the previous Friday, on 18 May it was decided that the league season would end in the same manner as the lower divisions. This meant Celtic were crowned champions for the ninth season in a row and Hearts would be relegated to the Championship.

Hearts, being the third biggest club in Scotland, were never going to take this lying down and their owner Ann Budge, who had been given the green light by the SPFL to head up a committee to discuss reconstruction of the leagues, threatened to take the SPFL to court. For a club which was struggling financially, as well as on the pitch, this was always going to be doomed to failure. Reconstruction was the only 'get out of jail card' Ms Budge had to save her club from the drop, but her proposal was rejected by the other teams. The question was: would she have been so vociferous if her team had been sitting second bottom of the table instead of Hamilton Accies?

This was a desperate time for Scottish football and all the clubs were suffering financially with no income coming in. I understood Ann Budge's stance, sticking up for her own club, but my opinion was, and still is, if there were going to be winners there also had to be losers. That is the nature of any sport.

As a football man I found it very frustrating not being allowed to attend matches and being unable to properly celebrate United's league triumph, by that I mean winning it on the pitch. Also, the bickering between some clubs, individuals and the SPFL had become increasingly tedious and had done nothing for the credibility of our game.

While all this was going on in dear old Bonnie Scotland, the rest of the 'big' leagues throughout Europe were desperate to complete their competitions. The clubs in the 'big four' of England, Germany, Spain and Italy claimed, in the interests of 'sporting integrity', their leagues had to be completed. Those countries had massive TV deals and they had to finish off their seasons as the financial penalties for their clubs by not doing so would have been huge. The difference in Scotland was that, being such a small nation, the TV deals here paled into insignificance in comparison.

What the countries hadn't considered was when their new seasons would begin and what kind of knock-on effect they would have on European and international fixtures.

As the coronavirus levels were different from nation to nation, lockdown restrictions were eased within separate timescales. The big four, in agreement with their governments, restarted their leagues at different dates during June. There was one condition for this to happen – all matches were to be played behind closed doors and televised live on TV. The biggest nightmare for any football fan – not being able to get to the game, share a few beers with your mates before and after, and the camaraderie which went along with that.

The 2020/21 Scottish Premiership season began on 1 August 2020, albeit behind closed doors. The SPFL had reached an agreement with their broadcasting partners, Sky, for every match to be streamed live and fans offered virtual season tickets.

What started as a book entitled *Tales from the Touchline* has ended as *Accounts from the Armchair*.

When will it all end?